FREUD, WOMEN, AND SOCIETY

FREUD, WOMEN, AND SOCIETY

J. O. Wisdom

Transaction Publishers
New Brunswick (U.S.A.) and London (U.K.)

Library of Congress Catalog Number: 91-13593
ISBN: 0-88738-444-7
Printed in the United States of America

Library of Congress Cataloging-in-Publication Data
Wisdom, J. O. (John Oulton)
    Freud, women, and society / John O. Wisdom.
        p.   cm.
    ISBN 0-88738-444-7
    1. Psychoanalysis.   2. Freud, Sigmund, 1856–1939.   3. Women–
–Psychology.   4. Sex (Psychology)   5. Bisexuality.   6. Androgyny.
I. Title.
BF173.W549   1991
155.3 – dc20   91-13593
                                                        CIP

Contents

Preface

This is not a polemical book.

There is much concern these days, some holding that psychoanalysis is a science, others that it is not. The answer is simple: it is *not a science*. It is in the same position as the studies on electricity and heat were in some centuries ago. All the arguments and passions, however suggestive, were left behind — but they had played a necessary part, though necessarily speculative — when the first real theories emerged. Thus electricity became a science in the nineteenth century as a result of the work of James Clark Maxwell (some would include Faraday; he had a lot of ideas that he didn't develop into a theory). Some theorems were known. Archimedes understood the truth about floating bodies (and some might say he invented the theory of hydrostatics). The theorem of the parallelogram of forces was invented by Stevin of Bruges, but there was hardly a theory of statics before Newton.

Psychoanalysis may likewise develop into a theory or it may not. Meanwhile for nearly one hundred years, its theories have been at a standstill, despite Freud's best endeavours. But now there may be a change. In 1983, in a review, I assumed without then knowing the new words — that is, I implied an *acceptance of — glasnost and perestroika in psycho-analysis*. Perhaps Professor Paul Roazen preceeded me. Roazen has written that "those who have wanted to challenge the official line have not had the publishing support given to the official powers that be" (Roazen in a review, 1990). And he had often remarked on the power of the self-renovating élite to block any deviance. Here is another who has constantly criticized the quality and nature of psycho-analysis Stoller (1985*b*). But between us, and perhaps with others, Roazen and I have declared *glasnost and perestroika in psycho-analysis*. This is a freeing development as it was for the philosopher, Berkeley, who in 1734 demanded "free thinking in mathematics." Even mathematics had its 'old guard' (as it happens, Berkeley was right and the old guard were wrong).

It has been said to me that my ideas are speculative. Of course they are. I may as well defuse this innocent criticism at once. Almost all psycho-analysic theory is and almost always has been speculative. Furthermore, all scientific thinking in its prescientific stages is speculative. So I do not apologise. Nor do I mind what is said against me. The social "sciences" or the human "sciences" must risk their necks.

The overall thrust of the book is to come to terms with Freud, to try to challenge Freud on the nature of woman, and to understand what is normally taken for granted – the nature of man. We are thus taken willy-nilly into where I want to go – the psycho-analysis of society. For we cannot tackle society without a reasonable understanding of the two pieces on the chessboard, women and men. I suppose one could say that this volume is an introduction to group psychology, though in that area we have got no further than tribal relations between men and women, homosexuality, and perversion.

I will end this part of the Preface by stressing the amount of labour, emotion, and dogfights that would have been saved if Freud *and* his classical followers had realised that psycho-analysis began anew in 1897 when it was first realised that unconscious Phantasy had taken the place of preconscious memory – so many writers give the impression that they never realised that *fact of history*.

I turn now to another topic altogether. It saddens me to have written a book without making central in it the work of Winnicott (though I am relieved to know that there is a first-class book about him [Phillips, 1988]).

My other, and perhaps graver, omission concerns Bion. I have written several papers about his work that failed to cover some of his important ideas; he requires a volume to himself.

Bion shares with Winnicott and Freud the realization of the importance of 'waiting for it'. Let the patient come to it himself. Bion's creativeness out of nothing was godlike: *ex nihilo scire fit*.

A further disconnected remark. The working of Bion's mind is best understood from a novel by Iris Murdock (1986), esp. part 2, in which an amateur psychiatrist runs through in his mind a whole host of things he *might*, but does not, say to a patient. Bion would choose what to say in the light of the patient's later associations.

I will now assume that there is no need in every paper or chapter to genuflect to Freud.

In *Part 1* I deal with Freud's 'leftovers' in a way I think he might have accepted. In *Part 2*, from a 1983 paper on "Male and Female" I sowed the seeds of what I call *androgyne*, which is then applied to Havelock Ellis and Darwin. In *Part 3*, this idea is developed in relation to women, men, and society. I do not expect this idea to be accepted at all; it is more likely that my book will be taken to have brought forth *rediculus mus*.

The reader will not find much about emotional horror in the pages of Freud or other analysts — an allusion to them will be all that time and space will allow, not the space required by a novelist. The awful extent these states can reach can best be found — not in Shakespeare, Jane Austen, or Thomas Hardy — but in the brilliantly elaborated descriptions given by Steven Zweig (1989).

It remains to thank those who have given much help in the preparation of the book. First is my wife, Clara, who prevented many mistakes and detected misfits, as well as correcting inept phraseology. She was very patient. Then some of my colleagues at York University, Toronto. Apart from technical points, they were always available for advice or other aid. One couldn't have better colleagues than Professor J. H. Haviangadi, Professor Ian Jarvie, and Mr. Michael Gilbert.

But I am particularly indebted to my publisher, for suggesting certain re-arrangements in the book, and for the judicious advice to omit certain parts that were probably redundant or for incorporating appropriate pieces in the text. Some of the suggestions came from the highest quarters, Irving Louis Horowitz, the head of Transaction Publishers, a man closely acquainted with what goes through his hands. Mention should also be made of the very trying work that faced Ms. Luckett in her largely successful efforts to bring order to the manuscript.

J. O. Wisdom

Wilmont House,
Castlebridge,
Co. Wexford,
Ireland.

Acknowledgments

I wish to acknowledge permission by the author and respective editors to reprint the following in whole or in part or to include parts of in a typescript:

"A Hypothesis to Explain Trauma-Re-Enactment Dreams," (1949). *The International Journal of Psycho-Analysis, 30*, 13–20.

"Testing a Psycho-Analytic Interpretation." (1966). *Ratio, 8*, 55–76 (previously broadcast by the B.B.C. Third Programme, 1964, 1965).

"The Diagnosis of Darwin's Illness." (1983). *Philosophy of the Social Sciences, 13*, 69–71.

"The Psychical Self of Havelock Ellis." (1984). *International Review of Psycho-Analysis, 11*, 413–4.

"The Concept of 'Amae.'" (1987). *International Review of Psycho-Analysis, 14*, 263.

PART I

Loose Ends Left by Freud

1

In the Beginning Was Freud

This book reaches far beyond the title into masculinity, normality, phantasy, and social questions. Still the actual title will serve if readers are told that these subjects will loom large. There is another difficulty for the author and the reader, because none of these subjects develops in a straight line independently of the others. The answer to this obstacle lies, I think, in discussing each of them in small amounts. Then after each, or some, has been aired to a certain extent, it may be possible to survey the scene reached, and to decide which one needs further development at that point.

Every modern development naturally and inevitably begins with Freud. Everything I now write is animated throughout by Freud even if I differ from him *toto coelo*. So I no longer think it appropriate to genuflect on all occasions. It is no longer necessary to defend Freud — or not quite. His enemies are, so to speak, vulgar Freudians, and the answer to those who have 'slick' criticisms of him is to read *his* work. Yet it has to be admitted that he may not be understood even by those who have read all his work, perhaps even more than once, and perhaps been analysed for years into the bargain. I know of a few who have understood their Freud very well indeed. Freud himself. Ernest Jones. James Strachey. I think

Melanie Klein and Helena Deutsch. Presumably Anna Freud. Probably one should include Popper. There must be many others. There were 'the old timers' who were formed into a ring, and some outside the ring such as Balint. At one time I considered that I myself understood Freud. Having read nearly all his work long ago, all but four papers, I believe I no longer trust my own scholarship, so readers are asked to forgive me if I write about difficulties, problems, and the like without expecting me to go back to the fount for backing.

I think I should begin with some remarks about Freud. I have not read the numerous books about him, even the biographies, that have been published during the last decade or more. I believe that, in order to get some grasp of psychoanalysis today, one should be familiar with the very early work, the pre-analytic, which began with Breuer and Freud.[1] The reason is simple. He (or they) discovered or invented — shall we say 'lit on' — such basic ideas as 'resistance' and 'displacement'. Perhaps others, but these will suffice to teach that there were basic insights in the earliest days and that these are still alive, and used by all including non-Freudians. This work was 'pre-Freudian' or better 'pre-psycho-analytic' in that hypnosis and the pressure method and even the free association development, important though that was, did not recognise transference as a therapeutic instrument. Psycho-analysis began with the recognition and the use of transference, even though it was ill-understood for a long time — in some of its aspects for over twenty years up to which only the positive form was made use of (the negative, insofar as it was noticed at all was something to be got rid of). Though now followed by the negative form, the positive transference is still a vital part of psycho-analysis.

There is, however, one other feature of pre-psycho-analytic therapy, which I believe goes unrecognised. That is free association in the *presence of a listener*. My conjecture is that various forms of non-analytic therapy, and to some degree psycho-analysis itself, owe the benefit they sometimes confer on a patient to the mere fact that a miserable patient has someone to listen to his misery. Pre-analysis was born because Freud (I do not exclude Breuer) recognised that his patients were in trouble. Case reports for a long time have given the impression that this has been forgotten (though

I recall hearing a highly distinguished analyst reminding a group of analysts that one must not forget that patients come to analysis to have their symptoms removed and that that should remain a goal of an analysis — for it became the current outlook that analysis was a method of research, and an intractable case came to be regarded as a 'research case').

One of the great discoveries, or hypotheses rather, of pre-analytic days occurred in 1897 when Freud came to disbelieve in the truth of the astonishing string of what would now be called child-abuse phenomena. He had traced back by the pre-analytic methods a large number of cases of hysteria to rape or other forms of trauma in childhood. He came to believe these traumata had not really happened, but that the *pre-conscious* fantasy of them had occurred. The patients' memories were not lying. They were now recovering fantasies, and it was one of the greatest advances made before the full development of psycho-analysis, and imported into psycho-analysis from pre-analysis. In psycho-analysis it became additionally important because with the invention of dream-interpretation, it became a natural source of neurosis to look not only for conscious traumata but also for unconscious traumata. So with the advent of positive transference in the early part of the 1900's, psycho-analysis was born — not fully fledged till the 1920's, but well under way (Wisdom, 1984).

A word should be inserted here about the insidious attempt by Masson (1986) to show by dubious arguments (for a more adequate discussion the reader is referred to my review [Wisdom, 1986] or to Rycroft [1984]) that Freud never changed his mind in 1897 or thereafter, from his earlier belief that traumata always occurred in reality to the belief that they were nearly always phantasies — which he announced in 1905. Masson thus made the incredible accusation that Freud was a liar. A more honest man than Freud has scarcely walked the Earth (unless it be Abraham Lincoln or Ludwig Wittgenstein or Karl Popper).

I do not propose to go into this further here except to remark that the later work of Freud and the more recent work of those two great Freudians, Melanie Klein and Wilfred Bion was based on the reality of phantasy. (This remark, to obviate nitpicking, is not intended to refute Masson. It is intended only to point out an important way in which psycho-analysis has developed.) Psycho-analysis has now become the transference-analysis — or transference-interpretation — of free-associations and of unconscious phantasies. It only gradually became clear to analysts that unconscious phantasy had become the basis of psycho-analysis. It was clear from the beginning in Melanie Klein, but we can now see that it was clear in Freud from a very early time.

Do we now know any more than that mastermind, Aristotle? Do we know anything more about the human being than Socrates? I am inclined to reply, "nothing". But I suppose we should not exaggerate, i.e., when not overstating neither should we understate. About knowledge as a whole, we got some approximate knowledge with Newton, then a great basis for development with Darwin, some amazing illumination from Marx and from Maxwell, and a most profound development and failure from Einstein.

But what have we learned from Freud, adding in Melanie Klein and Bion? We have learned the importance of ambivalence in human nature, and the unbelievable ways we have of handling it, e.g. by splitting plus projective identification, etc. (Freud himself did not go beyond 'repression'). Then from Jung and Aristophanes the peculiarities of gender-identification. Freud, further, discovered — though he did not make the most of it — the significance of the unconscious and in particular of unconscious phantasy. Those two discoveries are enough to keep social scientists busy for many decades, perhaps centuries. If I feel somewhat disappointed with my own work, I reflect that it was a worthwhile endeavour to have understood to some extent the achievements mentioned above (my understanding of Maxwell's equations is not very wonderful).

In my opinion Freud was unlucky in his early colleagues. Many of them were able, Ferenczi, Abraham, Jones, etc. But there was a problem. His followers either agreed with him or disagreed — or partially agreed. Whichever they did was wrong, i.e., unacceptable. To be of his calibre they had to be different, to disagree in large measure. There are two difficulties about this. Freud lacked one vital quality — to accept and even learn from those who disagreed. The other way was to merge Freud's work with theirs, perhaps into a new synthesis. No one tried this out.

This last alternative was open only if those with really new contributions were of Freud's calibre. Creative people like that do not ripen like blackberries.

When do we expect the next Einstein, or Shakespeare? We cannot do anything to promote such a being. But we might learn not to get in the way. The first maxim for a doctor when prescribing is to give a medicine that will do no harm. Similarly with education. There is an authentic story about Einstein when he had a position as a teacher in a secondary school. He went to see the principal one day to complain that the mathematics curriculum should be changed because it destroyed originality. He was sacked on the spot. Better was the enterprise in Trinity College, Dublin, usually a profoundly conservative institution. It appointed Sir William Rowan Hamilton, who had been made Astronomer Royal of Ireland, to the Professorship of Astronomy while he was still an undergraduate. Voters take your pick. Remember responsibility to satelites.

Note

1. Here I am in agreement with my late friend, John Klauber (1987).

2

The Female Castration-Complex

Freud's two greatest mistakes were: (1) the castration-complex and (2) his theory of female sexuality.

They belong together as will become clear. The castration-complex — still adhered to by the majority if not all analysts — insofar as men are concerned was a product, and a natural developmental product at that, of the family triangle of father-mother-son. To make this more explicit, that triangle, whatever one may think of it, rests upon an idea of genius, the Oedipus Complex. Its plausibility should be noted first. It is a common observation that, save in special circumstances, little boys prefer their mothers and little girls prefer their fathers. This is not evidence for the Oedipus Complex but a natural though tortuous consequence of it. Freud was concerned, however, not with preconscious effects such as these but with the unconscious underlay. What he theorised was that boys feared castration by the father who would not tolerate their rivalry for the mother. In this theory the mother was simply a passive snare, the danger of whom lay in her being overwhelmingly sexually attractive to her son. This was a purely passive ingredient of the situation. But it evoked a terrible reaction of threat in the father, who was felt to have all the might of Jehovah or Zeus or

Siva. Total rebellion would mean playing the part of Satan. So the son usually compromised. In the unconscious compromise, the son gave up his lust for his mother and might bestow it on any other womanly figure (except the sister who was also taboo), and in return he could have some degree of his father's powers — identification and surrogate satisfaction, growing in his footsteps, and having some activities that were a compromise-formation with some elements of identification and some elements (not too risky ones) of rebellion. It must be emphasized that all these factors are unconscious. If it is found bizarre that a son should lust after his mother, it must be remembered that Freud meant all this in raw terms which, if they could not be faced consciously, had to remain unconscious. Failure to understand this makes for enormous difficulty in understanding Freud — and for irrelevant criticisms.

It was the same, *mutatis mutandis*, for the little girl. But only in certain respects. In certain important respects it was very different. Based on the sex instinct — which Lorenz as well as psycho-analysts would accept — Freud postulated, not unnaturally, a psychical representation of it, which was sexual lust, clearly visible in lots of men, and dignified by the name 'libido'. At this, even somewhat elementary stage, Freud had to make some theoretical leaps. One thing he wanted, reasonably, to account for was neurosis, for it was realised that not only women were 'hysterical' but also that *men* suffered from neurosis. This was a serious dent in the male armour, especially when Freud learnt from Charcot that even men suffered from hysteria. Without that discovery men might have been allowed the dignity of suffering from obsessional neurosis. The second thing to be accounted for was the large amount of social activity that betrayed no signs of sexuality. In the future special social ways may be arrived at to explain it. Freud, however, thought it was due to 'sublimation' of sex. He and his followers had no difficulty in explaining tennis playing, mountain climbing, reading, knitting, and so on as sexual sublimations. Some things did not really fit. So for these Freud had his alimentary-sewerage theory which had its own sublimations. He had to invent a whole new 'ball-game' to connect this with sex. Let us not take this up now, but return to the third item Freud was faced with — women's sexuality.

This has always been a contentious issue. For in Freud's day Victorianism had spread over Europe, and to many people it seemed that women did not have sexuality — at any rate not in that raw form in which some men have always displayed it. Although Freud of recent years has been accused of many shortcomings, he never doubted that (unless it was thwarted in some way) women by nature had a vibrant sexuality. How was he to handle this within the confines of his theory of libido?

Perhaps his theory of penis-envy arose thus: the woman has no organ for initiating sexuality. So, having come across a male with a penis, she thinks she once had one and that it has been torn away from her. Thereafter she has a castration-complex, which stems from an illusion, a phantasy. Likewise she develops an envy, not of the male as such, but of his penis.

'Penis-envy' has become a tiresome war-cry of feminist movements — which should forget it. The theory is widely recognised to be almost totally fallacious. One of the greatest women analysts of the 1920's who earned a place beside Melanie Klein and Freud, Helene Deutsch, was the first, while still a pupil of Freud's (Deutsch, 1925; 1930a [originally *Zeitschift* (1930)] 1930b, 1932; 1933; 1947) to point out the error. She held that the *generalisation* was untrue, but that penis-envy was to be found in some measure. It probably was true of the hysterics (my presumption) Freud had treated (assuming there were any). But Helene was very balanced. She contended, very reasonably, that penis-envy was a natural consequence of excessive masochism, i.e., that it was a secondary matter, but she never agreed with Freud that it was a 'normal' and inevitable development in a girl. Freud's view prevailed, with Anna Freud along with the Viennese and some British analysts, as the internationally accepted truth. It still survives with few dissenters, in orthodox psychoanalytic circles. Deutsch's criticism was followed by Karen Horney (1924, German, 1923) who usually gets the credit, but influential support came from Jones (1927) who mentions Horney though not Helene Deutsch. I do not vouch for the priorities and possibly Horney was first, but she did not go into the matter in depth, whereas Deutsch was concerned with the whole domain of women's sexuality. Naturally Melanie Klein was also involved. So I think the matter may be regarded as closed (closed insofar as any controversial matter is ever closed) — on Deutsch's terms, that the general theory of Freud's of penis-envy is totally false though as a symptom hinging on another psychopathology it is to be found. As a postscript I will add that I have know the occasional woman who I thought undoubtedly had penis-envy, being into the bargain highly vociferous about the theory. She was in analysis, and I have little doubt that her analyst battered away at it with assiduity though little effect. I have also heard as well-known analyst give a paper in which she described in detail her efforts to track down the effect. In the end she found it in a bizarre factor carrying no conviction. Perhaps the patient accepted it (whatever that means as a conscious contribution), might one say 'out of war weariness'.

In short penis-envy *can* be a symptom, but when it is, it is better explained in a way that is different from envy of the penis.

3

Sublimation

It should be clear from the foregoing that Freud offered more than he could deliver, and not only about female sexuality. The castration-complex in the male was not only a gross generalisation which there is no means of substantiating, but further it required a whole theory of symbolism which is itself a collection of generalisations about numbers of symbols for which virtually no evidence has ever been published.

It is easy to think that a walking stick is a phallic symbol. It is not so easy to follow the symbolism of the staircase or the umbrella. Freud, Jones, and others may well have been right about these matters. I think, however, they should all be regarded, not as hypotheses, still less as established, but as great seminal ideas like those all the known sciences have sprung from. We mainly hear about the great scientific hypotheses that have succeeded. We hardly ever hear about the seminal ideas that gave them birth. Freud's reply about the walking stick and so on would undoubtedly be that they fitted (maybe were justified by) his clinical experience. What we need is carefully stated vignettes of that experience showing what lay behind his connecting the symbol and what he said it symbolised. For instance I know of a case in which a man dreamt of his penis growing into a giraffe. This at least can be taken seriously. In all this time the only clinical writing on this subject known to me is a paper by Segal (1986).

Let us suppose now that the requirements for symbols can be met and pass on to sublimation which strongly resembles symbolization yet is greatly different from it.

Broadly speaking, a symbol (usually though there are other forms) manifests or is a sublimation of sexuality in a way that is not clear to the eye. For instance dancing—ballroom or ballet—would symbolize or be a sublimation of sexual intercourse. Possibly including all manner of qualifications, e.g., reluctant pursuit, determination, winsomeness, flirtatiousness, offer without a promise, yielding (this is intended not to be complete nor even a competent composition). Tennis would symbolise rivalry—the element of sheer play might require separate discussion. Mixed doubles might represent rivalry between the Montagues and the Capulets, with steps through the boundaries of aggression and hate. Men's doubles (or women's doubles) would seem to stand for 'ganging up' against others of like sex. Football would seem to be a sublimation of homosexuality. Cricket is harder to place. Perhaps it is a gentlemanly form of friendship which recognises foes in friends and friends in foes—a gentlemanly form of ambivalence.

When we go on to boxing we reach a different form of sublimation, namely (maybe not of sex) of aggression. Archery seems to represent plain aggression.

There are many other activities that seem to be complicated forms of sublimation, which may not seem far off from those mentioned. Architecture may be considered a form of nest-building. Aeroplane designing might well be, as Freud would have probably claimed, a form of phallic activity, perhaps normal, perhaps rapacious. Mathematical activity may be a curious, ego-function way of envisaging the world (see Hattiangadi, 1987). The priesthood, whether Greek, Hindu, or Christian, may be a representation of power, without ostensibly inflicting hurt (or sublimation of sadism, to use classical terms). The army clearly represents killing, defence being a cover for it (called rationalisation in the trade). Colleges stand for (I suppose but do not feel very sure about it) cornering the market in truth and preventing the rabble from gain-ing access to it, at least when it was regarded as the road to power. Systems of government seem to have been means of keeping people in their place (a superego derivative).

With sublimations of the sexual drive culminating in concrete, or of containing aggression within (Darwinian) bounds, of a questionable superego derivative of the sexual drive, of the lust for power. But that is not the end.

We can see possibilities in the alimentary system, which would be different from those above. Irrigation of the land would fit the idea of sublimation of the alimentary canal, requiring constant renewal and removal of the water supply, and constant evacuation of the drains (small intestines) into sewers (large intestines with an occasional clearing out of the septic tank or ditch [an enema]).

Freud himself regarded the human sewerage system of mankind as a development different from that of the sexual drive. His colleague, Abraham (1922) called it the 'anal phase', which Freud accepted. Jones (1927) added many details by attempting with some plausibility to show that many character traits were derived from it. I have heard Stengel in a teaching seminar complimenting Jones on his achievement, saying there must have been someone in his family life with a wealth of such traits, as Jones had given such a fine picture of them (Jones, 1948). This work led to a caustic comment by the late, and somewhat lamented, philosopher, C. D. Broad, who called anal erotism Jones' "family pet". The anal phase — I will postpone discussion of the Abraham-Freud theory of the three phases — beyond remarking that it has largely disappeared from psycho-analytic case histories, perhaps to their detriment as I claimed in a recent paper (Wisdom, 1984), for I consider that a large amount of modern civilisation can well be understood in terms of the anal-phase. Americans should easily understand this since almost every second word they use is "shit".

Enough has been said to ensure the plausibility of sublimation. But our examples have shown that, if there is such a mechanism or set of mechanisms, the net is wider than sublimation of sex. Ranking, one does not know whether equally or not, we have found sublimation of aggression, sublimation of power, and sublimation of our sewerage or alimentary system. Freud attempted in his libido theory, to account for these, or 'reduce' them to, sex derivatives.

It was very ingenious, but was it true, even plausible? I do not think many analysts, even the most classical, would endorse this now. But they never seem to comment.

Still the problem is more basic than that. Could all these supposed sublimations not be explained each by separate causes, could they not be severally explained by a variety of sources? Freud, from the point of view of scientific tradition, was right to be monistic in this matter. There is no way of supporting this other than by showing that a unitary theory will work (or to be scientific by showing that a unitary theory leads to some irreparable false consequence). I will now turn to a form (Freud's form) of this.

4

The Libido Theory

Freud, up against the Victorian era, rightly was impressed by the importance of sex in human life. Breuer had a hand in getting Freud to see what he had not fully noticed (Sulloway, 1979). Freud was aware of the ontogenetic and phylogenetic importance of sex. Breuer and Freud began their work by finding the peculiar role sex played in their patients' neurotic disabilities. It was an obvious assumption that there was a sex instinct in man (also held at much later times by the great animal biologist, Lorenz, 1967). But biology could not — at least not then — do Freud's psychological work for him. So he postulated a psychical correlate of the sex instinct which he called the sexual drive, the most important if not the only psychical representative of the instincts. All this is reasonable enough and would probably be acceptable to all who had any real experience of the world. But Freud sought to reduce all psychical representations of the instincts to that one drive. This important generalisation will be considered in due course, but the task now is to investigate what other ideas the sex drive carried along with it.

According to Freud, the sex drive was the flowering of what came to be called 'sexual libido': The reason for broadening the scope of the drive was that it was necessary to account for, not only ordinary sexual lust, but also neurosis (which by now Freud believed with some evidence could be accounted for in terms of sexual libido), and also the extraordinary achievements of mankind, which we have discussed under the label of 'sublimations'. He thought many of these, if not all, could have sexual roots traced in them (though we have had hints that many sublimations had different roots).

So Freud had the beautiful theory — and it was a great theory — that sexual libido had three outlets: normal sex, neurosis, and sublimation.

In my opinion, based in part on the work of Melanie Klein, the neuroses — even the original ones, i.e., hysteria and obsessionality — had other roots as well as sex. Moreover, Freud, though he made a bold essay (Freud, 1905) failed to come to grips with homosexuality and perversions (Wisdom, 1988). Further, there were the psychoses which became tractable only by the pupils of Melanie Klein, the most notable of whom were Hanna Segal (1951), who was the first to analyse a schizophrenic, and Clifford Scott (1946), the first to analyse a manic-depressive (carried out before the war). There were other 'Kleinians' who tackled the psychoses such as Bion (1967), Rosenfelt (1965), Meltzer (1968), and a small handful of very brave analysts. Most analysts would not touch a case and probably not many Kleinians would. (It is not entirely correct to name Scott thus: but he was trained by Melanie Klein and thought largely, with whatever reservations, as a Kleinian; but he was 'his own man' and not accepted by the Kleinians after a time as a Kleinian. It is only proper, however, to add that Freud and the classical analysts regarded the psychoses as outside the scope of psycho-analysis.

Thus there can be no doubt that the libido theory failed to do more than the work Freud required of it. Perhaps incapable even of doing all Freud required of it, we are still faced with the idea of sexual libido and how much validity may be attributed to it.

That there exists universally sexual libido seems to be inescapable. But equally there seem to be other forms of libido — aggressive libido, alimentary-sewerage libido, and the drives of fear and hunger (Lorenz, 1967). Let us leave it still open whether some of these are derivatives of or components of sexual libido. For there is a further point to be made about sexual libido. Even in its own domain it has to be interpreted more widely than simply lust, for its coverage has to span such ancillaries as nest building and preening. This may be done in the way Lorenz has indicated.

Jumping this hurdle by passing it back to an ethologist, we have to look into Freud's phase theory (actually Abraham's, 1922).

Like all Gaul the person/self/ego was divided into or evolved through three phases. The first was the oral phase. Freud said a little about it but not much: he regarded the baby's tie to its mother as oral – basically and almost completely. So libido was oral libido. The dating of its length is somewhat uncertain, but I think the early Freudians looked on it as lasting for almost eighteen months or two years. Then began the 'anal phase', given some momentum by Freud and written about in detail by Jones. This occurred when the libido 'passed' into a concern with the rest of the alimentary canal or sewerage system, when the baby took a great interest in its faecal products, and probably would, if allowed, have played with or made bricks with its faeces. The phase was regarded as libidal because in it the baby displayed what analysts thought – and they were probably right – was ecstatic pleasure. The phase lasted on Freud's earliest view till the age of five, but later classical analysts have reduced this to about the age of three and a half. This stage if successfully passed through was succeeded by the 'phallic phase' which if it had a smooth passage would lead on to adolescence.

The transition from orality to anality in the baby consisted mainly in the development of an interest in the world around us. (So one can see with some justice that the world created by man has an anal root.)

The subject is further complicated by another division like all Gaul: the id, ego, and superego. This highly insightful classification must have been dimly present to Freud's mind but he did not formulate it till 1923 (Freud, 1923). The 'id' was simply sexual libido under a new name, and always totally unconscious. The 'ego' was for Freud conscious and the person's way of relating to his outside world. It was modified by implication and explicitly by Fairbairn (1952) (see Wisdom, 1946) to have an unconscious element as well as a conscious one. The 'superego' was the keeper of one's conscience and its ideals, and also most importantly the conscience as a terrorist of the self/ego/id. This also was modified by implication by Melanie Klein and explicitly by Fairbairn (same references) to have an unconscious element. One's conscience would be mainly conscious, unless we want to include in it a kind of 'warning signal' from the unconscious part.

Freud's mind was undoubtedly 'all of a piece', and what he did not consciously reach has to be fitted by us into what he had already reached. So I would hazard that the id represented all libido, oral, anal, and phallic, which all analysts are now agreed were obscure at the edges, merged with one another, and anytime under frustration usque recurrit. The ego fits in as nearly as we can hope with the anal phase, cleansed to a certain extent (small?) by the promptings of the superego. The superego does not fit smoothly anywhere. I am inclined to suppose that it belongs with the anal phase—in which cleanliness and orderliness begin to be learned. Surely it is from the anal phase that the superego, in the company of the ego, derives its torturing power. That is the best I can do to fit the pieces together. Incidentally it is worth pointing out what Freud appears to have missed: that the child on discovering what comes *out of* the anus must at some point wonder what can be put *into* the anus.

The libido theory, however much we may want to or have to modify it, was a great piece of thinking.

5

Libido and the Anal Phase

Freud clearly looked upon the libido as the most basic element in his psychology. We may rightly wish to understand its relationship to the instincts, but here there is another problem so basic that it has never been clearly delineated. Nonetheless it has properties assumed by Freud, and has been clearly handled by Abraham (1922). It comes about thus.

In a couple of years or so the baby gives up some of his interest in oral satisfaction as he becomes more interested in his excreta. Abraham agreed with Freud that at that period the baby takes an active interest in his faeces, and Abraham called this the anal phase. It was a kingpin of early analytic discussions and case histories.

But the libido is not set aside. So Freud and Abraham saw that the relationship between the libido and the anal phase was a central matter. The question was not explicitly posed, how does the libido or part of it become *transformed* into an anal form? And why is some of it not thus transformed?

We might try to answer the first of these as a one-body problem. This was undoubtedly the approach by both Freud and Abraham. In outline it would go like this: there was simply a sensory change in the taste, smell, feel, and accompanying sounds, all to the ba-by's satisfaction. The baby might notice some changes in the libidi-nal feelings; and other properties would be markedly different. Some of these would remain libidinal. But the baby might notice that he could not now exercise his accustomed control, such as he had when being able to take a pull at the breast on demand; and he could not always produce some faeces at will. We are thus led to answer the second question. For the baby when frustrated in these ways might hark back to the times when he had full control, i.e., he would remember the bliss of the oral-libidinal time. Seen this way, development involves a loss made up for by memory.

Nowadays, great numbers of psychologists of development would see the whole matter differently—as a three-body matter. Viewed thus the baby transfers his interest and valuation largely because of the attitudes taken by his mother. This hardly alters the picture. Much would remain as before insofar as a revaluation of the libidinal qualities is concerned. Frustration, which under the maternal pressure of toilet training might be greater than in the two-body version, and therefore leave a stronger yearning for the purely oral-libidinal time of satisfaction on demand, with-out the necessity of delay in getting a similar satisfaction in the anal phase.

At this point we can see the value of Doi's (1989; 1990; cf. 1963) concept of 'amae'. In other words if the toilet training has not been too severe, the baby would emerge with a relatively benign form of ambivalence. It is desirable, however, to explain more about 'amae'.

Doi has brought out the remarkable fact that 'amae' has no translation even in an Eastern language. But still more remarkable are its properties. It means demanding, also controlling at one's own behest, but strikingly also identification through merging). All three components can be present when the baby 'amaerues' the mother. So the baby can make a demand on its mother, be aggres-sive about it, and yet empathise with its mother. In this way ambiv-alence is present from the beginning but without being over-whelmed by any one component nor therefore overwhelmed by splitting. Doi's concept explains the pressures on the baby and on the mother at one stroke. I think Doi is right in supposing that if Freud had had this concept available it would have made his task of understanding the psychology of infancy much more tractable. In particular 'amae' would smooth the transition between the oral-libidinal phase and the anal phase. For the baby's annoyance with his mother is offset by merging with her.

What one may glean from the foregoing is that, while frustration and poor motherly handling may lead to all sorts of disastrous consequences, disturbance in the anal phase is likely to prove damaging in its own right.

Currently Loraine A. Gorlick and B. Bail (1989) are doing striking work on the anal phase, the message of which is that toilet-training, so often thought of as a simple development, is likely to lay the foundation, unless very sensitively handled, for many disturbances later in life. They draw attention for the first time to aspects of the matter that have hitherto been totally overlooked. Thus the baby does not know he has made a production, is kept from knowing it; and when eventually he is put wise to this he is not told why his faeces are put in a pot and taken away instead of being given to him to play with. The ground is laid for all sorts of illusions in consequence. It will take the baby years of upsetting experience of the real world before he can understand many happenings in the world, which in themselves seem so odd. Much social behaviour is fully understandable in terms of his childhood faeces and his mother's control of his pot. Particular consequences of importance are that the baby will learn that some good things are bad, some to be shunned, others to be vilified, and so on. One consequence worth mentioning straightaway is the widespread belief by little girls, pointed out by Helene Deutsch, in the cloacal theory of birth, which has probably led to much frigidity. This needs much greater elaboration, but we must await the publications of Gorlick and Bail, who have added considerably to the knowledge gained by Freud, Abraham, and Jones.

It seems reasonable to suggest that Freud was often right in his view of the repression of the oral-libido—where we might now understand the repression as being due to pathology in the anal phase.

Appendix: The Concept of 'Amae'

Dr Doi (1971), who has promulgated this concept, is of renown in Japan, and well known in some quarters of America, but somehow does not seem to be sufficiently acknowledged in the West, i.e., Europe. What he has found is that there is in Japanese an ordinary word, 'amae', with no equivalent in any other language, Western or even Eastern. The word, in its common or garden use, means basically 'clinging on to'; and Doi, who is a psychoanalyst, considers that Freud would have found his early theorizing easier if he had had this term instead of narcissism and object-love, and the convolutions that ensued. 'Amae' is both behaviour and affect.

This meaning of 'amaeru' implies that the object clung to is a willing receptacle. So 'amaeruing', which originates in babyhood, is clearly object-relational from the beginning.

Not surprisingly 'amae' is not confined to the state of clinging. It carries a note of demandingness or wilfulness, of having one's own way.

Doi is not content to stop at being a training-analyst and psychiatrist. As a student of literature and history, he is concerned with peoples, i.e., groups, and with society; he throws much light on the group-psychology as well as the individual psychology of the Japanese. He is able to illustrate 'amae' in many situations after babyhood among adults in ordinary life situations, and also in social conditions as with student unrest.

In its sense of confidently expecting succour, the nearest translation Doi has been able to find is the conception stressed by Balint of 'passive object-love', but he objects that in the West this would tend to be taken in a homosexual sense (as indeed Freud did take it). The only other similar mention he found was given (early sixteenth century), as referring to passive 'love', which included elements of gratitude and shame. If Japan is to a certain extent a society with a basic underlay of sense of shame, the Western man by contrast has wiped out shame, gratitude, and passive love, and in consequence has developed Western 'freedom', self-reliance, and individualism.

Anxiety, Doi regards as a consequence of being unable to

amaeru. More generally it would seem that what used to be called 'neurotic' colloquially—a bevy of symptoms as might be found in a hypochondriac, or characteristic of the classical hysterical patient studied by Breuer and Freud.

In addition to *unquestioning demandingness*, which I think covers both clinging and having one's own way. Doi draws attention to another component of 'amae' which he locates in *identification*—not that they are equivalent but that identification develops when amae is *not* satisfied. Here Doi is very close to Freud who saw identification as the baby's first tie with its mother. I would suppose (subject to correction) that in this context what is referred to is *introjective identification* (though it may be that projective identification is also involved). This third component clearly embraces the other two—for identification would provide a substitute for clinging and also for doing as one wants.

Japan also has many other interesting terms; but they are all translatable—not like 'amae'—unique and peculiar to that language.

The question now arises as to what difference 'amae' might make to Western psychoanalytic theory. Classical analysis found itself in tortuous problems over early object relations. Freud discovered narcissism, understood as a love-relationship towards a mirror-image of oneself. (He also had to distinguish between primary and secondary narcissism, though the latter is not a problem.) But primary narcissism (which also had to be distinguished from anaclitic object relationship) gives rise to the question of how the ego transforms its self-love into object-love. The idea of 'amae' obviates this difficulty altogether, since it presumes that the baby is born with an attitude conducive towards 'amaeruing'—which indeed is phylogentic as well as ontogenetic—and one must suppose that it is of evolutionary survival value. Doi (like Freud) considers it biologically rooted, though he does not, so far as I know, go into the matter of instincts or Lorenzian equivalents.

'Amae' is an ego-attribute, and would dispense with the sharp distinction between the ego and the id. It very soon and very easily attracts superego feelings of guilt.

Unlike narcissism it would seem that 'amae' could be interpreted clinically at a very early stage in analysis.

Touching on a different area, it is even possible that the concept would have cut the ground from under the petty war between Freud and Adler.

Summary

In Japan Dr Taceo Doi, a training analyst of considerable standing, has discovered that Japanese contains a unique word, 'amae', with no equivalent in any other language even in the East. It consists of at least three connected meanings. It applies to the psychology of babyhood, to adults, social psychology generally, and the psychology of the Japanese in particular. Though there are other significant terms in Japanese and contributions to psychoanalysis, this would seem to be the most important, or at least one of the two most important. The author also goes into its psychology.

Reference

Doi, T. (1971). *Amae no Kōzō Kōbundō. Tokyo. Translated as The Anatomy of Dependence.* New York: Harper & Row, 1981; several editions & reprintings, most recent, 1985.

Power: Nietszche and Adler

Perhaps Freud's greatest bungle of all was to neglect *power* and fail to fit it in with his libido theory. Adler made too little use of his ideas, trying to make masculinity consist of being the power position, failing to develop a sociology of power. The world is, after all, a powerhouse.

Though Freud appears to have read Nietzsche, he made little or no use of that ill-appreciated philosopher. Perhaps this is understandable in that it is extremely difficult to put Nietzsche's various insights together. The same is unfortunately largely true of Adler. Adler's personality and ambition were, I would suppose, a misfortune. But Freud could have made better use of him than to force him to resign from the early group of analysts.

Adler was at bottom a sociologist, but he didn't write a sociological theory—indeed if he had he would almost certainly have crossed swords with Freud even before Freud's work on group-psychology had appeared. It is the greatest pity Adler missed this opportunity. Instead of going down in history as a major sociologist, he has tended to become regarded as a rather dumb psychoanalyst. He seems to me to have lacked the necessary metascientific discipline to marshall his ideas. I will now try to mention some of his insights. For this I am indebted to Mauricio Kuperman (1979).

Adler held that man is essentially creative (Kuperman, 1979, 124). I would think this should characterize normality, and that neurotics are rigid. Adler, however, regarded neurosis as fluid, e.g., that a person might change easily and often from one syndrome to another (*Id.*). Freud tried to explain everything as stemming from conflicts. But he could not explain sadism and masochism in this way. Also he could not explain the element of domination, which was basic to Adler (*Id.*, 127–8). Adler maintained that man was a social rather than an instinctual animal (*Id.*, 129). Particularly important was his contention that aggression was created rather than discharged (*Id.*, 130) arising from frustrating experiences. He agrees with a psychologist called Ellis that our emotional reactions (one reaction or another) depends on how we see or interpret the circumstances confronting us (*Id.*, 1933 citing Ellis, 1962). Adler saw the importance of ideas, especially of 'world-views' (*Id.*, 142–3).

Thus Adler appears to have been sociologically minded, with a surprising emphasis on creativity as inborn. He seems not to have made the most of the fact that ideas have to be seen as socially rooted. He laid great stress on the social element of *domination*. This is as near as Adler comes to Nietzsche. It seems to me that this adds up to a significant contribution. Also, though the anal phase is not overtly mentioned, it would be accepted by virtually all psycho-analysts that all of these ideas would be rooted in the anal phase, though domination might begin earlier.

But it is no easy matter to integrate power into libido. Unless we do, however, the Freudian engine is left without a cylinder or two.

Never having been within a mile let alone a light-year of power, I lack analogies to clinical data such as a psycho-analyst would have in his background. I hear about power in the news — when I listen to it. I have seen a small extract of it in the universities. Perhaps predictably I think at once of my version of masculinity and femininity, and I hypothesize that man seeks power to establish his masculinity. But not in the sense of lust or being a successful womaniser. It is more like a question of Wotan's having his way. (If this is a suitable example, it should be remembered that the ultimate power lay with Fricka, his wife, who with one outraged moral decision and its consequences for Wotan's families, the Wälsung and the Walkyre, she wrought the final disaster, the destruction of their home including Fricka's home, with the tidal wave over Walhalla).

There is arguably a connection between power and oral libido. I think this could be formulated without too much difficulty by a Kleinian, power over the mother through hurting the breast and in other ways. But I do not want to press this.

Where I think power really does come in is in the anal phase, through the expulsion of faeces at untoward moments or the irritating retention of them. Toilet-training may be strongly resisted leading to a lengthy battle between mother and child. I cannot guess whether this battle would be more acute if the child were a daughter or a son. Possibly because of the girl's original identification with the mother and good babyhood, together they would make adjustment easier.

Be that as it may, the most important point to emerge for this book is that power would be a vital component of the libido in the anal phase. I think Freud, Abraham, and Jones could have seen this — to the advantage of all parties.

6

Narcissism

One of Freud's greatest ideas, which has so far escaped my net, was *narcissism*.

As Balint (1952) has made clear, Freud's pronouncements on the subject were confusing. There is still no satisfactory theory of narcissism, though the subject has attracted several psycho-analytic authors. The prevailing classical view began with a distinction between primary and secondary narcissism. The latter was always simply vanity and was thought of largely in feminine terms, the female vain about her appearance, looks, and so on, males being vain about their position, achievements, such as takeover bids, excellence in sport (though it would be fairly generally agreed that Anthony Eden was vain in the sense of his looks). So far it is quite simple. But Freud thought that secondary narcissism must rest upon a primary form. Primary narcissism was conceived to be a form of libido, focused in some way on the self/ego/personal libido. It was usually expounded in terms of the myth of Narcissus who fell in love with his reflection seen in the water. This will not serve, however, because it so clearly represents the secondary form.

Before trying to make sense of primary narcissism, we should first consider whether Freud really needed the idea. He seems to have thought he did, for the narcissistic neuroses became contrasted with object-relational disturbances. To this end he distinguished between auto-erotic, i.e., self-love, and love of an object (something personal). He thought, very reasonably if wrongly, that the baby began by being auto-erotic, and that it had, to be normal, to break through this barrier to form relationships with other people and with the outside world. In view of Melanie Klein's work, and the revision of Freud by Fairbairn, and my own considerable doubts about libido-theory, there is here a theoretical problem to which I have attempted on two occasions unsuccessfully to contribute (in papers given to the British Psycho-Analytical Society and published in their *Bulletin*). And there is a clinical problem which seems to be leading to a Kleinian solution. At first Klein held that object-relations were present from the beginning of extrauterine life. Later she weakened her position to the first week or so, in which case the problem of how an evolution from a one-body state to a two-body state knocks at her door as it did at Freuds', though perhaps less noticeably. The study of intra-uterine life would seem to support the probability of relationships of some sort which had their beginning in the womb. Even if this transition happens on the first day of life or later, it is a problem how this takes place.

Whichever view prevails, there is the abiding question of narcissism, though the formulation of the question would be different according to the date we settled for. But I think we can say that for Melanie Klein and Fairbairn there is no need for the idea of primary narcissism. In any case the theory of neurosis has undergone much scrutiny and some revision since Freud's time. It should be mentioned that Freud thought of the psychoses, at least schizophrenia, as involving primary narcissism. But the successful treatment of the psychoses already touched on in chapter 4 goes against a theory that attributes them to narcissism. I am inclined to think that Freud was led on by his own metaphor—hydrodynamics, the flow of a liquid from a centre outwards, and at some point turned round and inwards towards itself, which is the essence of narcissistic libido. The net result of my, admittedly rather poor, enquiry leads me to disown the idea of primary narcissism.

In summary, perhaps we could provide a usable meaning for narcissism: namely an attempt to establish a person's place in the world. Viewed thus the question would become part of the problem of identity.

One of the best treatments of the subject is by Doi (1962).

7

Freud's Classical Structure

At some point it is only natural to say something about *The Ego and the Id* (Freud, 1923), including the Superego.

With doubt cast on the idea of libido, implicitly by Melanie Klein and explicitly by Fairbairn (see Wisdom, 1954), one has to see what if anything is left of Freud's great structural theory. Fairbairn recognised at least three structural entities. He renamed them badly, and I have tried to devise a better nomenclature. Fairbairn was throughout an object-relational psychologist. Why Melanie Klein never took the same plunge no one has explained. I suppose she wanted to minimise the difference between her view and Freud's. What Fairbairn called the 'libidinal ego' I have named the 'libidinal lobe', to try to emphasize that the libidinal element was an important part of the ego. Further this lobe would have a conscious aspect as in ordinary sexuality and also an unconscious element to do the work of Freud's 'primary process'. The ego would remain the ego except for overt recognition of its conscious — everyday life functions — and its unconscious part consisting of forgotten memories, items not relevant at some moment such as how many pieces of toast one had for breakfast. The superego Fairbairn endowed with the harsh part of the personality — what is usually thought of as the superego — plus ideals and anything else that lacked a home. Again I have divided this into an 'aggressive lobe', largely unconscious, but also a part that is conscious, and what is usually regarded as one's conscience, mainly conscious though not completely. So Freud's neat tripartite division becomes six components (love and hate, love and hate for the father, love and hate for the father and mother combined — Wisdom, 1984). This need not, however, prevent us from using the time-honoured classification as an approximation or a shorthand.

Fairbairn has not been sufficiently recognised for his emendation of and advance on Freud.

8

The Oedipus Complex

I would suppose that the topics now opened up could be seen as culminating in the Oedipus Complex, and I think that is how Freud would have viewed most of them. But it is not a simple fitting together of components in a jigsaw puzzle. His handling of homosexuality and of bisexuality do not really fit at all. Again his threefold structure whose outstanding component was the superego came a good deal later than the Oedipus, for, as I have pointed out, something resembling it was always present to his mind from pre-psycho-analytical thinking. Moreover the components of the Oedipus, *including* the superego, were virtually all present from early days.

It is easy to see the castration-complex, sublimation, the libido theory and narcissism all building up in layers of his mind at more or less the same time and finding their niche smoothly in the Oedipus Complex. The order in which I have presented them in preceding chapters would not be the way a logically minded psychologist would put them together if he were trying to present them in the form of an axiomatised system. But, if we think of Freud as having his ideas at different times, first developing one idea, though at the same time being dimly aware of the other ideas, then we see his thinking as a whole rather than as a congeries of discrete ideas. However much of a scientist and intellectual he was, he was surely above all things an intuitive thinker.

We are in real difficulties, however, over bisexuality. His attempt to treat perversions as neuroses-through-the-looking-glass ("the negative of the neuroses") really failed to give psycho-analysis a way of handling them at all. And I doubt whether he can ever have been satisfied with his view of them. Added to which is the lack of clinical papers that gave the remotest hope of therapeutic progress with them. As will be seen later the very possibility of progress very possibly depended on the broadening of psycho-analysis by great women analysts, and on giving up the castration-complex for women. True, these analysts used that complex when it suited, but never, it would seem, as the *fons et origo* of a disorder.

So what position are we to give to the Oedipus Complex as the centre of the whole psycho-analytic theory, accepted by Melanie Klein, Helene Deutsch, followed up by Scott, Bion, Melzer and others?

A further part of Freud's ingenuity is to be found in his theory of the outlets for sex. The sexual urge is grounded in what he called the "libido". The three outlets for the libido were normal sexual activity, sublimation, i.e., an outlet of sex hitherto unrecognised, and *neurosis*. So in one fell swoop Freud had explained normal interests and neurosis. This was ingenious. When 'penis-envy' in women had to be given up, Freud's theory of neurosis was in jeopardy.

In both sexes, derivatives had to be latched on to the Oedipus Complex, to which he gave separate treatment.

Sublimation is developed as far as it can reasonably be pushed. But I think it cannot work unless it is attached to another fundamental factor, the anal phase. I have gone to some trouble in chapter 4 to see how anal erotism can be connected with libido. I will indicate my critique of Freud on bisexuality below, have dealt with his classical personality structure, and touched on the idea of libido and his theory of the phases. What I think we are left with is to handle bisexuality in such a way as to bypass the Oedipus.

The natural way to begin is to consider Klein's shunting the Oedipus Complex backwards to the oral phase. Whatever method there may be for testing Freud's theory at the phallic level could be used at the oral level, that is to say, in the case of a patient with little language, the analyst could test a clinical interpretation by its consequences, the difference being that an adult's response would be verbal, the child's would be by further play. And the analyst would face the same requirement of predicting the defence in the child's play.

But we have not yet considered the Oedipal components. Freud leaves us with the positive component to the mother and negative one to the father. Freud knew full well that their opposites also existed, but he did not try in depth to integrate them into his theory. Since Klein on clinical grounds postulates a 'good breast' and a 'bad breast', the question has moved some way towards an answer. Moreover in the 'depressive position' around eight months, the good breast and the bad breast can be experienced as one and the same thing. In Klein's theory, however, they both tend to be associated with the mother, so we are left with the problem of how the father of a male child becomes connected with the bad breast. I think we may begin to answer this if we make the plausible assumption that the bad breast becomes hooked on by the child to the male part of the mother's personality. This would become possible in the depressive position when the child recognises the mother as a whole person and the breast as a whole object. Then when the father is recognised as a whole person and introduces the negatives of life, there is no real jump in transferring the notion of the bad breast to him. As an amalgam forming a combined parent figure, it would be easy for the baby to switch its feelings from one to another of the components of the Oedipus. After a while, somewhere in the first eight months, when reality had become to some extent real, we might expect the good breast to be fastened on to the mother somewhat more than to the father, because the mother would in fact be the provider. Not all the time, however, for when the father came to the rescue, he would be the holder of the good breast. With further growth, the good breast would then oscillate between the parents.

9

Interchange between Conscious and Unconscious

Given that the unconscious and the conscious are two quite separate domains, how can there be any relationship between them such as Freud requires? Freud speaks most of the time as if the unconscious never becomes conscious and vice versa. Yet at other times he speaks differently. Thus in his *Studies on Hysteria* he is mostly dealing with the conscious, but at times treats deeply repressed traumata as having been *pushed back* into the unconscious 'Unbewust' really means 'rendered unconscious'. The reason why there is more to the matter is that certain ideas, such as the Oedipus Complex or the Castration Complex give the impression of *never* having been conscious. And one often gets the impression that the aim of analytic therapy was to make the unconscious conscious. We might indeed leave matters in the position of the unconscious' always remaining unconscious, were it not that it is supposed to affect people's lives in ways they have never been aware of.

Moreover the development of the concept of phantasy with its ramifications could not go ahead without the unconscious. As that concept developed, especially in the hands of Melanie Klein, it was natural to think of the unconscious as a complex domain, capable of containing scenarios, not just simple wishes; plots and counter-plots. Our task is to see how any of this could come about.

Take as an example (adapting one of Freud's) an embarrassing mistake made by a lady in a group of women in Vienna. She referred to the number 606 instead of something else. If an analyst were trying to find out what she had in mind, he might collect her associations. It might remind her of something *black*. The 'o' might make her say nothing was the matter. Wandering on to other matters, she might refer to the behaviour of soldiers and to the fact that they like to *discharge* their guns, though some wounds fortunately healed. The analyst (or the patient) could then put some of this together and conclude that the unconscious was denying that anything was the matter, and that a discharge which might be healed by something black hinted at syphilis (at that time black mercury ointment was used). Thus conscious signs could be found, though never the whole from which they sprang. It really would need an intuition on somebody's part.

Generalisation of this procedure meant that the unconscious would often give itself away. But the reading of it—the interpretation—would need the sort of skill exemplified on TV mystery stories. If we look at Freud's continued list of theories we may be able to see his work as a long line of development of ideas mostly in him from the beginning rather than as isolated discoveries. Thus early on he had the notion of a 'censor', a term he never used but which Flügel used on his behalf, for a mental factor opposing unwelcome ideas or producing shame or sense of guilt, remorse, vain hopes, or something fraught with unacceptable social ideas. We can see this as a prelude to his much later idea of the superego, which surfaced in him 20 or 30 or even 40 years later as a synthetic piece of thinking. We must suppose that this kind of idea was always living with him. Less able students learn the components piecemeal.

The reverse operation would possibly come about like this. An unwelcome idea would be avoided in consciousness, and parts of it, and anything remotely resembling it or even part of it would be replaced by another word or syllable.

But I believe the unconscious can be more complicated. I recall an ingenious piece of work by the late Cecily de Monchaux. She gave a paper — probably her membership paper, she was a young analyst at the time, in which she attempted to state the unconscious counterpart of every remark made by her patient, it seemed very successfully. In this way she hoped to give a coherent scenario of her patient's unconscious. How far this is generally possible, even with non-psychotic or borderline patients, I do not know. I would suppose it to be possible with simple cases. I can see it as a goal to attain with a psychotic patient. But the difficulty would be considerable of distinguishing between a patient's unconscious scenario and the analyst's projected gap-filling material. Indeed I suspect there is too much of the latter even at present — I know of a case in which a supervisor filled in the conscious associations to an extent far beyond the reported conscious material. It would be an endeavour, however, worth pursuing, provided the analyst would give up his scenario at any significant sign of the filling's not fitting.

There remains a situation well outside Freud's original work in which he dwelt on all areas of mental miscarriages. Suppose a situation in which a person climbs up a ladder holding a tin of paint to do a small painting job. Half way up he realises he has forgotten to stir the paint and goes down to get the necessary stick. Then he proceeds. Can we give an account of the whole unconscious process of carrying a tin of paint up a ladder, plus remembering a bit late though not too late that the operation is more complicated than had been envisaged at first? It would all be easy if we fell back on the old out-of-date idea of a homunculus.

Perhaps after all a modified idea of a homunculus will serve. It would not parallel the original form of the idea of an entity that saw, perceived, remembered, etc. But it could be a synthesis of the emotions, which were not part of the original homunculus. This would enable us to manage the problem set by the step-ladder example.

What it all adds up to is that unconscious phantasy is a coherent set of emotions of an unconscious homunculus.

The word itself will no doubt damage Freud, which is a pity because it expresses effectively the notion he was driven to, epitomized by Susan Isaacs and put to great positive therapeutic and theoretical effect by Melanie Klein.

The treatment of the subject above may appear to be, or may actually be, inconsistent with a view I expressed in a paper only a few years ago (Wisdom, 1984). There I claimed that the 'unconscious' was a term like 'gravitation' in that the test for it must be hypothetico-deductive. From the gravitational equation one deduces Kepler's laws, the motion of the moon, and the tides, and so on. No attempt has been made to do anything similar for the unconscious. There is no formulated theory of the unconscious, so we must begin by making one or part of one. Suppose we consider "the unconscious causes of displacements of thoughts and feelings from unpalatable ideas to acceptable ones", for example feeling castrated by guilt to smashing one's golf club in vexation (I have often heard talk of such a nature and presume it has happened but I never came across an instance of it). This consequence cannot be deduced from the hypothesis of castration without appropriate conscious accompaniments.

I do not see how to provide a possible situation that could refute this hypothesis. Oddly enough it is easier to apply the condition of refutability to a very general tenet, such as the Oedipus Complex, and I have earlier elaborated this test (see Wisdom [1966] or shortened form of this [Wisdom, 1967]). We notice, however, that in doing this we are not testing the Oedipus Complex in all its generality, for all peoples at all times. It is a test of the *use* of the Oedipus in a *clinical* situation. It goes like this. We notice also that to adduce appropriate initial conditions, we ask the analyst to succeed in doing two things. One is to take note of whether the patient repeats the outline of the interpretation of the Oedipus just given to him in the same form even though he couches it in material that may seem to have no connection with the Oedipus. The second condition, and more important one, is that the new material should contain a *predictable defence*. Psycho-analysis holds that a patient's material always involves some defence or other. In giving the interpretation the analyst is not expecting the patient to see its truth. But if in his response the patient does so with a new defense, perhaps less adament, but mainly has the same form, then the analysis is making progress, for the Oedipus, with lessened defence, is showing that the Oedipus is not dominating him so severely as heretofore.

It is possible, though more difficult to achieve, that the hypothesis of displacement could be tested similarly.

That would seem to be as far as we can go in the question of testing at present.

Many clinical papers could be devoted to noting unconscious counterparts of conscious clinical associations.

10

The Theory of Phantasy

A survey of basic Freud, even critical and incomplete, brings up many questions, to some of which answers may be found. But before any attempt is made to relate, say, narcissism, castration-complex, sublimation, etc. to one another, there comes a surprising question which did not arise in Freud's time. His early work, as already made clear, arose out of preconscious traumata. In 1897 he discovered that the traumata, presumed to be due to childhood abuse, were delusional, that is, the seductions presumed to have taken place had no reality. Instead of giving up another failure for the wastepaper basket, he bravely, as Jones strongly emphasized, carried on. Not with false traumata, but with a new notion. What took the place of the false traumata was the *Phantasy* of their existence. Thus Phantasies were hypothesized as having the same power to generate neurosis as had previously been attributed to real traumata. This new conception was accepted in the analytic world and led to a flowering of psycho-analysis. As Freud's work proceeded, it led to a new view of neurosis, as rooted in Phantasy. But before long, as Freud began explicitly to distinguish between preconscious and unconscious, it became an unavoidable hypothesis that certain — perhaps all — neuroses had springs in the unconscious. These springs were often surprising Phantasies — not fantasies of the daydream type previously pictured. Also some of the analytic discoveries, notably, the Castration-Complex and the Oedipus Complex found a more suitable home in unconscious Phantasy rather than in preconscious fantasy.

This development not only enabled Freud to develop his ideas in a more powerful way, but it led to wholly new work, in theory and in practice, at the hands of Melanie Klein. Thus Klein should be regarded as the natural successor of what was there for the taking from Freud's conceptions of the unconscious and Phantasy. That she made the most of it is history, and much was added to her work by Clifford Scott, Hanna Segal, then by Bion, Meltzer, and others. Psycho-analysis had become the psychology of unconscious Phantasy.

The idea of unconscious Phantasy was first presented as a newly developed concept by Susan Isaacs, but her famous essay on the subject should be regarded as a pioneering effort, but it was poorly written and constructed and did not give an account of concepts and terminology but it got the matter going. Philosophers of science are apt to forget that pioneering floundering is a natural stage in conceptual development, as desirable as in a baby's first efforts to walk and to talk.

I do not say that Melanie Klein got all of her findings about Phantasy right, but she got some and made some bold efforts. Freud's settling for Phantasy and the work of the Kleinians certainly seems to me to have led to this view of psycho-analysis: that, differ as one may from every Freudian or Kleinian individual theory, one is a Freudian if one believes that the spirit of Freud animates all efforts to understand unconscious Phantasy. (I think that, had Melanie Klein been able to put the matter in some such way as this, he would have understood.) Unfortunately his original followers do not yet seem to have seen the full importance of Phantasy.

Alas most advances open up a forest of new problems.

Psycho-analysists by and large have displayed little interest in or capacity for the structural or logical relations between their concepts or hypotheses. So instead there has been some drawing up of combat lines or, if you prefer, 'political positions'. An American author did collect in one volume various writings on Phantasy, but it did not prove fruitful. Recently, however, a London analyst has done better. As a result of teaching seminars she held at the British Institute, she (Hayman, 1987) produced the best piece of writing so far on Phantasy. She did not, however discuss the idea in general, as she was concerned with the 'controversial discussions' that took place during the war between classical analysts, Kleinians, and some others. She also gives us a sniff of the nasty atmosphere that prevailed and the bad manners some displayed. But some made a genuine attempt to clarify the situation or the controversy.

First Hayman notes Freud's own view, which was wish-fulfilment imagery, and she remarked that all analysts would agree with this so far, but added that Isaacs aimed at extending the notion. Klein saw Phantasy as being unconscious. Freud would have accepted that. But I doubt whether he would have regarded unconscious Phantasy as absolutely basic or agreed that unconscious Phantasy constitutes the building material, as many psycho-analysts have it, of the whole subject — though I would claim that this is what psycho-analysis came to when Freud gave up the trauma theory in 1897. Now, in addition to being unconscious and representing the instincts, Hayman rightly says that Freud's view was hallucinatory wish-fulfillment, which was based on his and Ferenzi's idea of a primary introjection. This quickly led to the notion of Phantasy as defensive and as involving anxiety. Hence a new-born infant's instinct to suck implies Phantasy from the beginning. Classical analysts have never accepted this, however telling are the clinical illustrations — which are of course debatable in their own right. The classical view continued to stress auto-erotism for some time preceding object-relationships and phantasies. The addition of 'part-objects' to the babyhood scene did not really affect the argument. The dispute is over the question whether an early Phantasy is retained in unconscious memory — which also involves the cognate question whether the baby has an object-relationship to the mother (or breast) or simply reacts in a similar way each time the object is present. This would amount to whether the baby regards itself as a part of its mother. The Kleinian view like Doi's, also carries with it the hypothesis that the baby suffers a sense of guilt, and the beginnings of a conflict between love and hate. The classical view on the other hand presupposes correlations, such as one might attribute to a cat or dog. Hayman cited Jones as finding it beyond credence that the wish to chew up a breast should spring into being at the age of three or four (according to Wälder) without a preceding Phantasy.

Hayman went on to reveal the intense disagreement there was over the question of evidence (Hayman, 1987), and a query over 'retrospective inference'. Isaacs more or less saw the point, wrongly admitting that *all* Phantasies were inferred. Freud even had made childhood reconstructions from adult analyses — and he was criticised for it. Freud saw phantasizing as more complicated than hallucinatory wish-fulfilment. He never said some of the things Isaacs pinned on him, but it is not clear why he should not have said them, e.g. Phantasy-hallucinatory wish-fulfilment. His view of secondary processes may only need complicity in the Phantasies.

Hayman then distinguishes Phantasy and thinking (Hayman, 1987, 12–13). I do not see a difficulty here. We could see thinking as a make up of conscious or unconscious phantasies. Hayman has done a marvellous intellectual job. My sole criticism is her ignorance of historical conjecture. In it the past is not 'deduced' or 'induced' or 'retrospectively inferred'. A past event is a historical hypothesis from which when combined with relevant facts we can *deduce an observation in the present*. (See Wisdom, 1984b)

When all the dust has settled, I can find nothing untenable in the idea of unconscious Phantasy as unconscious wish-fulfilment. And this, while being obviously Kleinian, is Freudian all the way.

11

Trauma Re-enactment Dreams

Before Freud nothing — virtually nothing — was known about the human mind. What little there was can be found in Plato and in the works of the greater novelists.

I began by paying homage to some discoveries of pre-psycho-analytic days, not usually recognised as such in sophisticated circles. These go beyond displacement and even transference, giving a nod towards the importance of a listener. Freud also opened up the role of Phantasy.

This, in terms of contribution, would not amount to much viewed as propositions of psychology up to the turn of the century. Seen in terms of developments thereafter they are dynamite. It is as if Maxwell cut his electromagnetic equations in a stone on a bridge (which Hamilton actually did) and did nothing with them. Maxwell was not so remiss (nor Hamilton).

Freud's theorising was all of a piece. This fact led him on from the beginning to the end, a point which should be remembered by critics.

It led him into serious error, however, for it impelled him to try to adapt — most ingeniously — the castration-complex to women. I think it did much to prevent the development of psycho-analysis.

Psycho-analysis was developed by women almost at the cost of schism. The error has been to a large extent put right, largely by a new use of Freud's ideas.

The obvious direction in which to turn for a way ahead would be Klein's. She held that the Oedipus Complex arose at, or very soon after birth. I think it makes more sense of her work to claim boldly *at* birth (though I think it would make just as good sense to place it in the last part of gestation when the cortex and brain are formed). Here, however, I am not concerned with this thorny question of timing, but to arrive at a structure sufficient to take account of the probable components that must be included if the complex is to make sense.

In my paper on psycho-analytic theory (Wisdom, 1984), I mentioned six components required for the Oedipus.

Although one can reasonably see Freud as regarding all the other matters discussed above as connected with or stemming from the Oedipus, one item defeats me utterly. I cannot understand how he could have regarded bisexuality as having any close connection or indeed any connection at all with the Oedipus Complex. Presumably Freud effected a bridge between the father and the breast.

12

A Dream Problem

Because dreams occupied Freud in the early stages, I will deal here with an old problem, though it does not fit in easily with the foregoing topics.

It seems best to present this by reprinting an old paper, the first I wrote on psycho-analysis (Wisdom, 1949), as that paper virtually says it all. Freud as I explain did not see most anxiety dreams as incompatible with his theory of wish-fulfillment but by 1930 he did admit one and only one exception — dreams, like shell-shock cases, that re-enact a trauma. I called these trauma-re-enactment dreams. When I handed it in to the *IJPA*, Rickman, one of the editors, commented on all those hyphens and the Teutonic style. I agreed but could not think of a way round the clumsiness; I still can't. I can but apologise. (If one wasn't particular about connecting the noun "trauma" to the next word by a hyphen, *that* hyphen could be dispensed with (an American sub-editor would probably delete it). Likewise when "re" is inserted before a vowel in English it needs a hyphen. So I have let the phrase stand.) Perhaps the rest of the composition would be heavier than I learned to write later. I have not altered an argument that seems a bit too easy-going or to jump hurdles. The overall intention of the paper was to mend a breech in Freud's theory of dreams, to show that it continued to be compatible with the theory of wish-fulfillment.

A Hypothesis to Explain Trauma-Re-enactment Dreams

Need-Fulfilment

Freud's fundamental and revolutionary hypothesis was that dreams are wish-fulfilments, but the general problem arises whether we can understand all dreams in this way.

It will be convenient to write "need" instead of "wish". The need involved is recognizably a need, in the way in which one may recognize a need in another person or in oneself. This does not necessarily preclude the use of "phantasies of which a person, awake or asleep, is unconscious" as equivalent to "need", though some would prefer to distinguish these and say that only when a need is directly felt as such can it manifest itself as a wish. The reason why the change of terminology is convenient here is that the general result becomes easier to express: for it is natural to use "wish" as an abbreviation for "pleasure-wish", so that a wish is either a pleasure-need or the acceptance of a pleasure-need; but here we shall have also to take account of needs that are unpleasurable or lead to unpleasure.

The obvious difficulty about the hypothesis is that anxiety-dreams do not fulfil pleasure-needs. To discuss this it is convenient to divide dreams into four classes: (i) those that are wholly pleasurable; (ii) those that are more or less pleasurable; (iii) anxiety-dreams consisting of punishment-dreams; and (iv) anxiety-dreams consisting of trauma-re-enactment dreams.

With regard to punishment-dreams, the criticism that they do not fulfil pleasure-needs has never impressed psycho-analysts, because they hold that it contains a very elementary mistake: the dream consists of a story in images and the image-story is called the "manifest content"; but what this expresses—the interpreted pattern—is called the "latent content"; and it is to the latent content alone that the pleasure-need is attributed. Thus the anxiety-dream has a manifest content in which the anxiety is regarded as a distorted product of a pleasure-need; for it is, of course, true that on analysing punishment-dreams we always find a pleasure-need, and therefore the old formula of pleasure-need-fulfilment is not incorrect.[1] But this failure to deal with the difficulty that anxiety dreams do not fulfil pleasure-needs: such dreams may be a product of such needs but do not *fulfil* them.

The situation is more complicated than has generally been supposed and must be examined more fully. The first class, consisting of wholly pleasureable dreams, contains those that are apparently undistorted in content, *e.g.,* some childrens' and explorers' dreams; it also contains some that are obviously distorted, *e.g.,* 'alarm-clock' dreams. In all these the manifest content is clearly the fulfilment of a pleasure-need. In the second class, there is some degree of pleasure-need-fulfilment but also some failure to fulfil the pleasure-need completely (or else some pleasure-needs are fulfilled and others not). Here there is only *attempted* pleasure-need-fulfilment (this concept Freud introduced, without pursuing it, in connextion with trauma-re-enactment dreams;[2] but clearly it may be applied more widely). We may now remark that what makes the attempt is not the manifest content but the dream-work. The pleasure-need lies in the latent content and the fulfilment in the manifest content — and this holds equally of wholly pleasurable dreams. With the third class the attempt is a failure. Thus Freud's original formula of pleasure-need-fulfilment, while giving expression to the profound truth that there is a need seeking pleasurable fulfilment, has a metascientific[3] disadvantage, because the dream (*i.e.,* manifest content) is *not* always a pleasure-need-fulfilment (nor can it be said to 'express' a pleasure-need-fulfilment, for it expresses only a pleasure-need and the fulfilment is only attempted). A revised formula, however, in terms of attempted pleasure-need-fulfilment is equally applicable to all three classes of dreams considered.

We may now turn to the question of what prevents the fulfilment of an attempted pleasure-need-fulfilment. The dreamer's latent content consists of a conflict between a pleasure-need and something else to which this need gives some displeasure or shock (the effect of which is, of course, softened by distortion). Now this factor may be of a vastly complex kind in comparison with the pleasure-need, but however that may be it is satisfied only by seemly ideas and shocked by others. One has only to recall one's experience of social life to see that men have a need to be punished:

> There are many such punishment tendencies in the mental life of man; they are very strong and we may well regard them as responsible for some of our painful dreams.[4]

We must go further: we must assert that this punishment-need always underlies dreams providing incomplete pleasure-need-fulfilment. This is not, of course, a wholly empirical statement: for it amounts to being an implicit definition of "punishment-need", implying that the phrase is used for all factors that interfere with complete pleasure-need-fulfilment. The role of the punishment-need in punishment-dreams, moreover, was recognized by Freud:

> For they merely put in the place of the interdicted wish-fulfilment the punishment appropriate to it, and are thus the wish-fulfilment of the sense of guilt reacting on the contemned impulse.[5]

The importance of the rôle of punishment-needs is enhanced by their origin. It is known, of course, that pleasure-needs have a childhood source, but there is no difficulty in seeing that the same is true of punishment-needs; as Freud says,

> one must attribute a traumatic character to infantile experiences as well.[6]

On the other hand, punishment-needs do not seem to play a part in determining the content of every dream — they are apparently not represented in completely pleasurable dreams.

The position, then, is this. We have noticed enough of importance about punishment-needs to warrant our describing dreams in terms of them as well as in terms of pleasure-needs or attempted pleasure-needs. We have seen that the concept of pleasure-need-fulfilment is applicable to the first two classes of dreams, *i.e.,* those that are wholly pleasurable and those that are partially so, but not applicable to the last two. The improved concept of attempted pleasure-need-fulfilment is applicable to the first two and also to the third, *i.e.,* those punishment-dreams that have pleasure-needs underlying them; but it does not appear to apply to trauma-re-enactment dreams—a point to be discussed later. By contrast with this, the concept of punishment-need is applicable to the last three classes of dreams, though not apparently to the first. *Prima facie*, then, there are both feature of fundamental importance and limitations on universal applicability to be ascribed to either concept, attempted pleasure-need-fulfilment or punishment; so that we shall not be relinquishing one of universal applicability in favour of one with less power by turning to punishment-needs for purposes of describing dreams.

The advantage of the new concept is that it enables us to replace the formulation. "Three out of four classes of dreams are attempted pleasure-need-fulfilments" by "All dreams are need-fulfilments"—where dreams of the first class are purely pleasure-need-fulfilments, those of the last apparently purely punishment-need-fulfilments, and those of the other two contain both[6a]. This is not to say that Freud's formulation in terms of 'attempt' is incorrect. The preceding discussion goes to show, on the contrary, that it is in large measure equivalent to a formulation in terms of 'pleasure- and punishment-needs'. But the latter has the advantage of making explicit one very important factor in the production of certain classes of dreams, namely the punishment-need, which is implicit and only dimly discernible in Freud's account. From the present point of view, it may be added, the common denial that a punishment-dream is a pleasure need-fulfilment is justified and not an error due to confusing manifest with latent content; for such a dream is the fulfilment not of a pleasure-need but of a punishment-need. And the profound analytic contention of a pleasure-need behind anxiety is not in the least put in the background by this; for the new mode of expression carries the implication, exactly as Freud's formulation did, that the punishment is directed against an unrecognized pleasure-need.

With regard to apparently purely pleasurable dreams, like those of an explorer dreaming of a feast or a little girl dreaming she was sailing on the lake on which she had wished to sail longer the day before, there is justification for holding that a punishment-need is represented in the manifest content. These are, after all, sophisticated dreams. The man has acquired a taste for civilized food—

this is more evolved than the taste for milk from the mother or what he can scavenge from nature. The child has learnt to find pleasure in sailing in a boat—more subtle than the taste for being rocked at the breast and so on. These sophistications are stable transformations of infantile pleasure-needs (known as "symbolization", "sublimation", and "reaction-formation"). In their turn, they may be seen to arise genetically from infantile pleasure-needs and punishment-needs. Thus even dreams of this class contain representations of punishment-needs in the manifest content: but the stability of the transformations involved makes it difficult to discern the punishment-need. And it is to this stability also that we must attribute the undistorted nature of these dreams. But plainly they are undistorted only in the trivial non-analytic sense of faithfully portraying real experiences: they are distorted in the psychoanalytical sense, every whit as much as any other dream, in that the content replaces the most primitive objects that give pleasure and mete out punishment.

It would therefore be justifiable to hold that in such dreams the punishment-need plays an important part. But clearly it operates at a deeper level than the one under general consideration: here the punishment-need contributes to the adoption of stable representations (symbols, sublimations, and reaction-formations): but once representations have become stabilized and adopted, the rôle of the punishment-need is to manipulate them. Thus at less deep levels the punishment-need helps to determine whether a breast shall be represented by an apple or a nectarine, but in the class in question its function is to enable the breast to be represented by anything at all other than itself. In the dream of sailing, though at a deep level there is a punishment-need directed against the pleasure for which sailing is a substitute (sublimation), there is no further manipulation of the manifest content; there is a maximum satisfaction of the frustrated need to sail. Frustration has no special rôle here; its function is as always that it *instigates* the dream, but it is not *represented* in the manifest content.

Because of the depth at which the punishment-need operates here, forming stable representations rather than manipulating the imagery, there is a sense in which it does not appear in the manifest content. For this reason it seems justifiable to keep the first class of dreams separate from the others; we may still regard them as wholly pleasurable dreams.

Trauma-Re-enactment Dreams

There remains the fourth class, the other subclass of anxiety-dreams, which may be called "trauma-re-enactment dreams". These are characterized by the re-enactment of a traumatic experience, and the dreamer awakes in a state of anxiety: typically one dreams of an actual scene from the past such as a bomb explosion. About them Freud says:

> So far as I can at present see, dreams that occur in a traumatic neurosis are the only genuine exception . . . to the wish-fulfilling tendency of dreams.[7]

His last word on this subject in 1933 was that such dreams might be regarded as *attempted* pleasure-need-fulfilments; but he did not regard this as saying anything essentially new.[8] (He added that the dream-work 'fails to operate': but this may be questioned, if only on the grounds that where there is no dream-work there is no distortion, and therefore the interpretation should be obvious — which it is not.) His general conception here is that these dreams constitute a limit case in which pleasure-need-fulfilment is equal to zero — *i.e.,* in effect that there is no attempt at pleasure-need-fulfilment.

The outstanding characteristics of these dreams are that they (1) express no discernible pleasure-need and (2) apparently contain no distortion.

I propose to pursue the hypothesis that there is nevertheless a pleasure-need and that there is a real attempt at pleasure-need-fulfilment. Now it is naturally taken for granted that the trauma-re-enactment dream expresses a punishment-need. But if there is no distortion, in the sense that the manifest content reproduces faithfully the traumatic experience, the supposed pleasure-need would have to be expressed by exactly the same manifest content. That is to say, the punishment-need and supposed pleasure-need would have to have at least a common aim — which would in fact be destruction. But one would naturally suppose also that the two needs would have to have a common object. What does this suggest? We do not find such dreams dreamt to their conclusion: a bomb explodes, but we are not told who is destroyed. Thus, if there is a difference of object to differentiate between the punishment-need and supposed pleasure-need, it does not appear in the dream. Unquestionably one object—that of the punishment-need—is the dreamer (or part of him). Now let us suppose that the dreamer's attitude towards the object of the supposed pleasure-need is such that he treats the object as if it were within him, occupying part of him or filling out all of him. Then we should have an answer to our problem: the supposed pleasure-need is one that aims to destroy some object (naturally a human being or part of one), taken to be one with the dreamer (or part of him): and the punishment-need is a need to be destroyed, in revenge for the destruction of the object. Thus both needs strive in the same way and can be expressed by the same means: they have the same aim and similar objects—their actions are parallel.

The hypothesis thus has three parts: (i) that there exists, as well as a punishment-need, a pleasure need, (ii) that these needs have a common aim, destruction and (iii) that they have a (nearly) common object.

Is it true, as Freud suggested, that the dream-work 'fails to operate'? This may seem to follow because the parallelism of the actions arising from the two needs prevents distortion. But in this context "distortion" refers to discrepancy between the manifest content and the actual perception at the time of the trauma. Now this is not the psycho-analytic meaning of "distortion", the technical sense of which is that the manifest content does not express the needs in a recognizable form. In general, of course, whenever there is distortion in the first sense, it occurs in the second sense also; so that if we find a discrepancy between manifest content and previous experiences we infer a discrepancy between the apparent needs of the manifest content and the needs in the latent content. But there is no reason why the concomitance should be universal. Hence, though trauma-re-enactment dreams lack distortion, in that they faithfully reproduce a traumatic experience, we should investigate whether or not there is distortion in the expression of the needs. The answer to this is simple. The dream may be the explosion of a bomb; but the latent content is the explosion of what the bomb stands for, namely the dreamer (or part of him), and someone else (or part of someone else) taken to be within him. There is therefore Condensation of these two objects and either Displacement from these two objects to the bomb or Symbolization of the object by the bomb. Hence the dream-work plays its usual rôle, even though not with the usual outcome of manipulating the imagery into some bizarre form.

It may be added that Freud's concept of attempted pleasure-need-fulfilment could be utilized even here, if desired: for the dreamer is attempting to fulfil — and largely succeeding — his need to destroy another person (or part of one). The need is unrecognized doubtless for many reasons, but a minor one may be that we are taken in by the absence of distortion in the trivial sense.

Just as any law of pure science, when it is applied in practice, has first to be expressed in a technological way, we can give the present hypothesis a clinical form. When a patient dreams of any traumatic experience, if this is more or less faithfully reproduced in the manifest content, the analyst could interpret: "This frightening experience you dream about represents a battle in yourself: you are trying to destroy something in yourself and it is trying to destroy you." What the object might be could be investigated in the usual way by means of associations to, say, the bomb.

The problem under discussion concerns the peculiarity of dreams that re-enact a trauma, but the subsidiary problem has not been touched on, of why such dreams are repeated again and again. It is doubtful, however, if there is anything unique in the repetition of trauma-re-enactment dreams, for other dreams can be repeated too. Still, there is a much greater tendency to repeat trauma-re-enactment dreams than others. The reason for this may perhaps be described by saying that most dreams merely give vent to one or two facets of the dreamer's conflicts but that the trauma-re-enactment dream expresses a cross-section of them. The story of a person's conflicts told in dreams is usually a story in several chapters and we require many dreams before we can understand the whole tale; but the trauma-re-enactment dream is apparently a short story, giving us not merely a facet or even the nucleus but the entire structure of the fundamental conflict. This may explain why an unpleasant experience is traumatic to some people: it portrays an entire conflict too faithfully.[9]

The Mechanism of the Dream-Work

The process of attempted pleasure-need-fulfilment is a means by which some pleasure is obtained that would not be obtained otherwise or by which some conflict is replaced by a pleasure. It is possible that the concept of 'punishment-need' will throw further light on some aspects of this process.

It is obvious that the processes of Condensation, Displacement, and Symbolization are ways of reducing the unpleasure of punishment-needs, though this cannot be elaborated without discussing ego-structure. We may admit the possibility of these processes of distortion occurring in a state of dreamless sleep. They may be conceived as operating in accordance with a principle of 'least action',[10] i.e., operating in such a way that the sum of energy expended during the interval in which they are active is a minimum. Moreover, though they have the function of reducing unpleasure, they may be conceived as operating even when only pleasure-needs are present.

So far, this is a description of activity that may be ascribed to the latent content, before a dream exists; only when the process of Perceptualization comes into play as well do we have a dream. Now the latent content of a dream has a different affect value from that of the manifest content; Perceptualization would have no function, i.e., a dream would have no function, if it merely expressed in hallucinatory form the latent content without alteration of affect. Consequently, however important the process of distortion may be for decreasing unpleasure, Perceptualization has a special part to play in furthering the aim of increasing pleasure; and with some classes of dreams at least, Perceptualization succeeds in this.

But punishment-needs also become perceptualized. Hence the aim of diminishing unpleasure by perceptualizing would not be achieved if Perceptualization fulfilled both pleasure-needs and punishment-needs at the same time. Let us therefore consider a hypothesis about this process.

Let us suppose that Perceptualization is a mechanism by which it is primarily pleasure-needs that are expressed in imagery. That is to say, Perceptualization would be primarily a process of forming pleasure-hallucinations. Then an 'internal environment' would be created. Now this process is not instantaneous. In the first stage of it, a beginning is made in expressing some pleasure-needs in some degree. The new environment thus created would provide satisfaction, so that the dream at this stage would be a pleasure-need-fulfilment. The aim would then be achieved of providing an environment without hostile or dangerous content and therefore an environment that would not goad the punishment-needs. But in the second stage, where the pleasure-needs were in process of being fulfilled in greater measure, the punishment-needs would be stimulated further and, through association with the pleasure-needs, would become perceptualized. Hence Perceptualization, though beginning by expressing only pleasure-need-fulfilments, would in the end express punishment-need-fulfilments as well. The end result, if reached, would be that the manifest content would mirror the latent content.[11]

This hypothesis about the time sequence involved in Perceptualization may be supported on the following grounds: firstly we find dreams in which the sequence is from pleasure to unpleasure, but rarely if ever the reverse; and secondly it is plausible to suppose that the infant's first hallucinations, which are precursors of dreams, are pleasurable.

The Mechanism of Sleep-Preservation

A sleeper may be disturbed not only by a physical stimulus, such as an alarm clock or some somatic, kinaesthetic, or visceral sensation, but by a punishment-need. He tends to awaken or enter a state of light sleep. Why should he not wake up? To answer this we may first ask why he should. To awake would alter the environment: it would replace the dangerous environment in which the punishment-needs were fulfilled by a new one where they are not goaded—just as a frightening drama loses some if its hold after the curtain falls. This way of soothing the punishment-needs by 'flight to reality' is opposed, however, by the need to sleep. This is a specific pleasure-need of importance:

> The wish is the guardian of sleep, not its disturber . . . the wish to sleep
> . . . must thus always be taken into account as a motive of dream formation,
> and every successful dream is a fulfilment of this wish.[12]

We might therefore describe light sleep as a state in which punishment-needs are stimulated while the need for sleep persists. In this condition the punishment-needs, not soothed by a change to external environment, nor by any change in the latent content, if we assume that the work of distortion has been carried as far as possible, can be soothed only by the creation of an 'internal environment'. This creation is the work of Perceptualization; thus this factor in the dream-work would have an important function. If, now, we allow the previous hypothesis, that Perceptualization begins by fulfilling pleasure-needs, we can understand that conflict in the latent content is soothed by a diversion consisting of a newly created internal environment fulfilling pleasure-needs. Since, however, according to this hypothesis the punishment-needs associated with the fulfilled pleasure-needs also become perceptualized, the end result tends to be reached in which the manifest content would mirror the latent content; and, as no other means are open for creating pleasure to prevent the punishment-needs from wakening the dreamer (except for the weak process of Secondary Elaboration), they wake him.

We might here admit the possibility of dreams passing from unpleasure to pleasure, if other sources of pleasure than those that goad punishment-needs can be drawn upon, thus creating an 'internal environment' with additional power to relieve the pressure on the punishment-needs. This possibility would explain the impression of having had a disturbed sleep and dreamt all night; and the process might well be the mechanism of Secondary Elaboration.

In the field of trauma-re-enactment dreams, pleasure-needs and punishment-needs are so closely associated that they are apparently perceptualized together. This raises the question, what function does Perceptualization serve here, where it only mirrors the latent content. In effect none. The existing mechanism would come into play in a hopeless attempt to preserve sleep by pleasurable Perceptualization – hopeless because the punishment-need would be represented in the dream almost as soon as the pleasure-need. None the less the mechanism would come into play because the pleasure-need would be perceptualized first, even though by a short head. One would expect such dreams to be of brief duration.

Situations of awakening may, then, be grouped as follows. (*a*) The dreamer may awake because of a physical stimulus. In the course of awakening he may satisfy his pleasure-need for sleep by having a pleasurable dream, though in the end the stimulus may prove too strong; or his pleasure dream may stir up a punishment continuation, which may wake him. (*b*) In the absence of a physical stimulus, the pleasure-need for sleep may become satisfied, but in the course of awakening, even though this may not take very long, some degree of need for sleep must remain, and the same effects may ensue – possibly it is here that we should expect to find examples of Silberer's threshold symbolism. (*c*) If he is awakened neither by a physical stimulus nor by satisfaction of the need for sleep, he can be disturbed only by stimulation of his punishment-needs. Here a diversion is created by a pleasurable manifest content, though this can serve only to give temporary respite to the sleeper.

It seems evident that the important factor in the dream-work connected with the need for sleep is the mechanism of Perceptualization. The mechanisms of distortion play only a subordinate part, in so far as Perceptualization would fail if they had not already been put into operation. This is not to say that they do not help to preserve sleep; but that is not the question being considered: the question is how the dream, *i.e.,* manifest content which is perceptualized, aids sleep.

It is worth pointing out that by means of the concept of 'punishment-need' we can avoid speaking of transforming anxiety into pleasure in a dream, in the sense in which anxiety has sometimes been conceived as convertible into pleasure; instead a pleasure source is utilized in order to create a new situation by creating an 'environment', thereby relieving the pressure of the punishment-needs. Moreover, the concept seems to throw light on the way in which pleasure-need-fulfilment is attempted.[13]

Summary

The general problem is whether we can understand all dreams, from those that are (i) wholly pleasurable, (ii) more or less so, and (iii) of an anxiety kind, to those that (iv) re-enact a trauma, as fulfilments of pleasure-needs. Some dreams do not fulfil such needs. If we claim that fulfilment is attempted, the attempt must be made by the dream-work.

What interferes with the attempt is a 'punishment-need' — and punishment-needs, like pleasure-needs, have childhood sources. The use of this concept, instead of 'attempted pleasure-need-fulfilment', enables us to describe all dreams in terms of need-fulfilments.

This clearly covers the fourth class, consisting of trauma-re-enactment dreams; the question is, however, whether these dreams also spring from pleasure-needs. Such dreams express no discernible pleasure-need and apparently contain no distortion. If we form the hypothesis that they do spring from an attempt at pleasure-need-fulfilment, a coherent account of them can be given. The absence of manifest distortion means that the supposed pleasure-need and the evident punishment-need are expressed in the same content, so that there is a common aim of both needs (destruction) and a nearly common object (the enemy object identified with the self, or part of it). Thus the hypothesis consists of three parts, concerning the existence of pleasure-need, common aim of pleasure- and punishment-needs, and (nearly) common object. Such dreams contain distortion, however, in the full analytic sense, for the object and self are distorted in expression by Condensation and by Displacement or Symbolization. Of this hypothesis there is a clinical application equivalent to an interpretation in terms of an internal battle'. The repetition of trauma-re-enactment dreams is a subsidiary problem.

This hypothesis therefore allows us after all to say "All dreams are attempted pleasure-need fulfilments."

It is necessary to enquire how the functions of the dream-work fit into this framework. A dream arises not from the mechanisms of distortion but only from Perceptualization. To account for the greater degree of pleasurable affect found in the manifest content than in the latent content, we form the hypothesis that Perceptualization begins with pleasurable material, but that unpleasurable material, being associated with it, becomes expressed somewhat later.

The aim of this is sleep-preservation. The pleasurable content is perceptualized in order to provide an 'environment' for the sleeper in opposition to a physical stimulus, external or in the body, and in opposition to the unpleasure of punishment-needs. This description holds also for trauma-re-enactment dreams, though the duration of pleasurable Perceptualization would probably be very short. The main weight of the task of sleep-preservation is placed on the mechanism of Perceptualization.

The fundamental hypothesis that dreams are need-fulfilments or attempted pleasure-need-fulfilments may be formulated as follows: *A dream or Perceptualization during sleep is either an undistorted Perceptualization of the fulfilment of pleasure-needs alone, or a Perceptualization of them distorted by Condensation, Displacement, and Symbolization and modified by Secondary Elaboration, in both cases to preserve sleep against disturbance by a physical stimulus whether external or in the body, OR a Perceptualization of both pleasure- and punishment-needs, distorted by the same distortion mechanisms, to reduce pressure from the punishment-needs by distortion of all needs and by initial Perceptualization of the pleasure-needs alone, with the aim of preserving sleep against disturbance by punishment-needs aroused by the unperceptualized pleasure-needs.*

Notes

1. Sigmund Freud, *Introductory Lectures on Psycho-Analysis*, London, 1943 (Vienna, 1917), p. 188.
2. Sigmund Freud, *New Introductory Lectures on Psycho-Analysis*, London, 1937 (Vienna, 1933), p. 43.
3. I propose the word "metascience" instead of "methodology", which lays the stress on method in the sense of techniques. "Metascience" has its parallel not in the old world "metaphysics" but in the word "metalanguage" of current deductive logic.
4. Freud, *Introductory Lectures on Psycho-Analysis*, p. 185.
5. Sigmund Freud, *Beyond the Pleasure Principle*, London, 1922 (Vienna, 1920), p. 38. *Cf.* Sigmund Freud, *The Interpretation of Dreams*, London, 1932 (Vienna, 1900), p. 514.

6. Freud, *New Introductory Lectures on Psycho-Analysis*, p. 44.

6a. It seems to me now that I allow the idea of 'punishment-need fulfilment' to be assimilated to wish-fulfilment too easily. It needs a postulate of 'guilty pleasure' or something of that sort, perhaps a theory of primary masochism.

7. Sigmund Freud, "Remarks upon the Theory and Practice of Dream-Interpretations" (1923). *Int. J. Psycho-Anal.* **24**, parts 1 and 2, London, 1943, p. 70.

8. Freud, *New Introductory Lectures on Psycho-Analysis*, pp. 43–4.

9. It is worth pointing out that neither the use of the terminology of "needs" nor the above hypothesis is intended to imply the existence of life and death 'instincts'; nor any hypothesis about instincts. The terminology arose through a routine metascientific examination of the customary way of expressing dream theory, and was developed for the sole purpose of explaining 'the only genuine exception . . . to the wish-fulfilling tendency of dreams'. That this hypothesis should emphasize the rôle of the destructive needs seemed to be required by the problem to be solved; it did not arise from a prior hypothesis about the death-instinct'.

   Perhaps it should also be added that the hypothesis in its present form neither asserts nor denies that punishment-needs arise at pregenital levels of development.

10. Freud held that the processes were carried out with the minimum expenditure of energy, which he naturally called an "economic" principle. But this omits the time factor, which, it would seem, ought to come in. The energy is expended over a certain time-interval, and what is minimal is likely to be not the energy at any one moment but the sum of energy expended throughout the interval. For this the concept in physics is known as "action", which has the dimensions of the product of energy and time.

11. This hypothetical process can be clarified if we accept Scott's cogent hypothesis (W. Clifford M. Scott, "Some Embryological, Neurological, Psychiatric and Psycho-analytic Implications of the Body Scheme." *Int. J. Psycho-Anal.,* **29**, part 3, London, 1948, p. 153, col. 1). He points out that, to gain satisfaction from a hallucination, part of the gratification situation must be destroyed. Thus, when an infant needs the breast, the breast may be hallucinated and there may or may not be a hallucination of sucking, but the sensation of sucking must be destroyed; for, if it were not, it would be unsatisfied and defeat the purpose for which the breast was hallucinated.

    It may be remarked that, to investigate the dream Perceptualization and derive it from the most elementary kind of hallucination, it would be necessary to establish a genetic connexion between punishment-need and frustration.

12. Freud, *The Interpretation of Dreams*, p. 229.

13. The present approach has a certain amount in common with the view recently put forward by Garma (Angel Garma, 'The Traumatic Situation in the Genesis of Dreams', *Int. J. Psycho-Anal.* **27**, parts 3 and 4, London, 1946). He gives convincing illustrations of the influence of traumas on dreams; and his chief conclusions are that traumatic situations are the source (i) of all dreams, not only those that re-enact a trauma (it is of course necessary to give a suitable interpretation of some children's and explorers' dreams, in which there appears to be no trauma, but simply pleasure-need-fulfilment), and (ii)

of the hallucinatory aspect of dreams — *i.e.,* what is here called the 'Perceptualization' is due not to pleasure-need-fulfilment but to traumatic situations. In short, the manifest content and the fact of being perceptualized are both due to trauma.

According to this view, while Garma agrees that dreams often express pleasure-need-fulfilment, he does not regard this as a universal characteristic of dreams. Hence there is no special problem concerning those that re-enact a trauma; we do not have to explain how they fit the pleasure formula because they do not fit it at all. The general explanation lies not in this formula but in the trauma, which he holds is sufficient to explain all dreams.

The development of this approach (Angel Garma, "The Genesis of Reality Testing: A General Theory of Hallucination", *The Psychoanalytic Quarterly*, Vol. XV, No. 2, New York, 1946) depends upon his hypothesis that all hallucinations, including dream images as a particular case, arise from a trauma, without *necessarily* being compensations or pleasure-need-fulfilments. The process by which they arise is as follows. Garma holds that an internal danger is easier to deal with than an external one, because the infant is helpless before an external danger but can repress an internal one. Hence, when confronted with an internal danger that is too great to control by repression, the infant regards it as external, simply because external dangers cannot be controlled; and this of course requires the danger to be perceptualized.

On this view of the genesis of hallucinations, the following comments may be made: —

(i) For Garma, repression has to operate before hallucinations can occur. A difficulty about this is that hallucinations possibly occur from the earliest weeks of life, whereas repression is likely to arise later.

(ii) His suggestion seems in one respect to be at variance with experience; for, if an inner danger appeared in the form of a hallucination, one's worst fears would be realized — there would be the feeling voiced by "It is really happening".

(iii) On the view that the internal danger is not felt as internal, it would be necessary to explain how this comes about — especially as, on his hypothesis, repression has been unsuccessful.

Let us suppose, however, that these objections could be satisfactorily disposed of, *i.e.,* that hallucinations are Perceptualizations of inner traumas, and let us return to Garma's account of dreams.

His conclusion, that both the manifest content of all dreams and the fact of Perceptualization originate in traumatic situations, is susceptible of two constructions. One is that traumas cause dreams without necessarily being represented in the manifest content. This was the classical view, according to which dreams were satisfactory fulfilments of frustrated pleasure-needs. But Garma clearly means something more (and this is where his view of the genesis of hallucinations comes in): since an uncontrollable internal danger is regarded as coming from without, the trauma is itself hallucinated. Hence the construction to be put on his conclusion is that traumas both cause dreams and are represented, however distortedly, in them — one of the contentions of the present paper.

What, then, is the difference between Garma's view and the one here maintained?

For him, a traumatic situation suffices to produce a dream without the aim of pleasure-need-fulfilment. The present hypothesis retains this classical aim as basic: the dream is due to pleasure-need-fulfilment, but the *need* for this fulfilment is due to the goading of punishment-needs. In other words the *dream* is due to the need for pleasure but the *need for the dream* (or need for the need of pleasure) originates in punitive factors — in the phrasing of Freud and Garma, the trauma sets off the wish-fulfilment tendency. The origin is the trauma; the mechanism, pleasure-need-fulfilment.

Our chief divergence of opinion arises over the mechanism of the genesis of hallucinations. When Garma's hypothesis is applied to dreams, it appears to lead to an unacceptable consequence. In the course of dreaming, on his view, the first image would be an image of the trauma; then, presumably, the mechanisms of distortion would operate, so that subsequent images would represent the trauma in distorted form. So far, this may be tenable — provided every dream begins with a most frightening image that we never remember. But the following difficulty arises. Garma holds that the trauma is perceptualized so as to make it like an external object, an he holds that external objects cannot be moulded at will like internal ones; but the application of mechanisms of distortion to dream images shows that such images are not treated as if they were external objects. Hence his view that dreams are internal traumas made to appear as external objects precludes the operation of the distortion mechanisms of the dream work.

These doubts cast on Garma's hypothesis may be due to misunderstanding and might disappear if he were to develop his view in detail.

PART II

Bisexuality

13

Male and Female

In *Part 1* I have dealt with Freud's "leftovers" in a way I think he might have accepted. In *Part 2* I plan to sow the seeds of what I call *androgyne*.

Bipeds can be divided (mainly) into male and female. This is usually done by a midwife who inspects the genitals, announces 'It's a boy (or girl)'; this is duly inscribed on a birth certificate, and the matter is settled for life. It is generally assumed, including by dictionaries, that a biped is exclusively one or the other.

When we leave the safe area of physiological definition and seek the social discriminations between male and female, we run into unresolved difficulties. Ernest Jones disagreed mildly with Freud on female sexuality and quoted a source of inspiration 'older than Freud': 'Male and female created he them'. (I, too, have somewhere repeated Jones's mistake.)

In a good many societies, including the British Isles up to World War I, there were clear social differences that could be depicted, without overlap. It is worth making brief allusion to these since the younger generations seem to think that the revolution in all such matters started only a decade or two ago—whereas, while it accelerated and peaked only recently, it originated more than half a century earlier. Time was when the man hunted, sat behind a desk, kept a maurauder at bay, punished the children, mended a leak in the roof; when the woman washed the children on occasion, prepared the food for cooking, cooked it, cleaned up after the meal, cleaned the living accommodation, put the children to bed, prepared the man's nightcap. Here there were sharp differences between men and women, social differences, sharp social-role differences. None was exchangeable.

But now? For some decades man can do each one of these things; if so, it is acceptable by the woman; it is acceptable by the community. To a lesser degree woman has been able to do and has done, each of the things hitherto done by man.

Consequently we can no longer tell by role whether a biped is a man or a woman. We are back with the anatomical differences — plus difference of strength. But no social role is a consequence. Social roles that were thought to be consequences are not — a man can nurse a baby with a bottle which he knows how to prepare. (But, apart from Zeus, no male has given birth.)

Psycho-analysis in its early classical days thought there was an *essential* difference between man and woman, and formed the hypothesis that the essential social differences were consequences of the essential anatomical differences. Thus man was a hunter, warrior, business rival, disciplinarian, because he had a penis. The woman cooked and looked after the hearth, looked after the children, soothed their hurts, because she had breasts. Man's roles are easy enough to see as sophisticated offshoots of the penis; the woman's as sophisticated offshoots of breast-feeding.

Since the non-anatomical roles have turned out after all these millennia to be exchangeable, the above derivations collapse — unless some curious rescue is possible. In fact we seem to be driven to two possible alternatives: (i) that the roles in question are not consequences of anatomy at all but have some other origin; and (ii) that the roles are consequences of anatomy, provided we introduce a further set of hypotheses. One of these might be that woman's penis-envy provides her with a *Phantasy* of possessing a basis required for man's social roles — the fantasy in this regard being just as powerful, or nearly so, as the reality of the penis in the man. This would no doubt be thoroughly acceptable to classical analysis ever since the time when Freud produced his theory of female sexuality based on penis-envy. However there is a further hypothesis to add (which would be widely unacceptable), that man has a fantasy of possessing breasts and womb (*part passu* with woman's fantasy of possessing a penis); which, of course, presupposes the hypothesis of breast-envy and womb-envy on the part of man. For brevity I will confine the matter to breasts.

It is worth spending just a little time on the extreme repugnance felt by the male all down the ages at such ideas as breast-envy, a Phantasy of possessing breasts, or anything 'womanish'. This has been anathema to the male to a much higher degree than the corresponding envy of the male that has existed in the female. The male has accepted the compliment; the female has accepted — or adjusted to — her second-class citizenship and thinks it is just a piece of male idiocy to want to identify himself with her — she being accepted by men and women alike as inferior.

But apart from this, man has apparently always had a huge problem over his machismo. Hence his breast-envy had to be sternly kept at bay. Man risks his manhood if he admits to having any form of womanhood. On the other hand the woman can risk pursuing male activities without fear of losing her femininity. I find this asymmetry baffling and can make only one tentative suggestion to explain it. On the one hand, if man tries to make his fantasied breasts productive, this would lead most easily to fellatio, which would be incompatible with penile insertion. Woman, on the other hand, with the Phantasy of having a penis, and its attendant activities, can also have the Phantasy of fellatio, i.e., in this case of giving suck, which is compatible with her possession of her breasts — not to mention that, through her fantasy she is in a good position to understand the man and control him, and so far as she falls in with his needing fellatio she provides an equivalent of sorts to vaginal suck. If the question should arise why man cannot put his fantasied breast to a parallel use, the answer would be that in man the fantasy is incompatible with penile insertion — masculinity — whereas in woman the fantasy works in the same direction as her femininity.

That is as far as I can go in trying to make the classical idea work by introducing hypotheses within the spirit of classical analysis (perhaps with Kleinian additions), in order to see social derivatives as understandable consequences of the anatomical differences between the sexes.

Now I begin to diverge. Two facts may have been noticed. One is that the social consequences are indeed societal — they are not consequences derivable from the bare idea of an anatomically male or female baby without some social set-up. The other is that woman, it is suggested, has a penile understanding of man, that is to say, can identify with him.

Thus there is an indication of man's identification with woman which is denied with the utmost intensity; and of woman's identification with man which, always admitted to some extent, is becoming more and more open. Woman has never been ashamed of her ancestry, Adam's rib; man has had no ancestry to call his own (unless dust) — till Melanie Klein suggested the breast. More than half the world's psycho-analysts find man's breast-envy as unacceptable as those members of women's lib who repudiate the idea that their essence lies in penis-envy.

Of recent decades there has been, I think, a gradual change of attitude among psycho-analysts, and I shall return to this later. I now propose to take seriously both that man has something female at his core and that woman has something male in her origin. This is in tune with a striking statement by Stoller (1975):

> . . . an anatomically normal male can become masculine and believe himself male, or feminine and believe himself female, either outcome growing from his family's psychodynamics (p. 36, cf. pp. 38–39).

If this should give the impression of going back to the first decade of the century, when Adler held that man demanded mastery and woman failed to get it, when Jung found in man what he called the 'anima' and found in woman what he called the 'animus' (female and male principles characterizing the other sex), why then let us go back and try to make the most of what psychoanalysis unfortunately let slip through its fingers. Indeed the idea goes back before Jung to Plato who got it from Aristophanes, though spoken in jest, a theory of both homosexuality and heterosexuality; leaving aside the twofold male and twofold female, the third species, which was androgynous, was split down the middle, and the male half spent his time seeking the other half to complete himself (and the female half similarly) — here was a valuation not a denigration of the complementary portion.

Let us note first one of the factors introduced above to help us understand woman's appreciation of man's activities as derived from his genital anatomy and appreciated by her as having the fantasy of possessing a penis. This hypothesis presupposed social male activities; for the things that he does that have traditionally marked him out as a male; however much they vary from culture to culture, in whatever culture they occur are societal. Thus we have been able to construct — or complete — the classical idea of penile derivatives only by seeing man and woman in a social relationship. And this is where Jung began, while Freud took unto himself the enormously difficult task of seeing the social relationship as constructed from anatomy (or as reducible to that anatomy), in terms of a one-body psychology.

What, then, if we begin the other way round and see the primary relationship as a gestalt of man and woman, and proceed to ask what components that may involve? The possibility opens up that a neurosis (or worse) in man or woman may turn on a sexual inadequacy of one of the partners — and also that it might turn on something else. By now nearly all analysts must have come across people who are severely neurotic or near psychotic but whose sexual functioning is excellent. (True, Freud held that neurosis went back not on flaws in adult sexuality but on childhood sexuality; but this is not relevant because he held that a person with a disordered childhood sexuality could not attain normal adult sexuality.) Hence we have no alternative but to seek the basis of psychopathology in something wider.

I look for such a wider basis in the coming to terms by a man (or woman) with the female (or male) aspect of the self. Certainly this involves the sorting out of gender-identity, as Margaret Mahler and also Eleanor Galenson have found. But they do not say in what gender-identity consists. So we have a difficulty in specifying what a man is when he is part female and in specifying what a woman is when she is in part male.

It is natural to look at primitive division of labour. Man, true to Darwin, was bigger and stronger, for attack and defence, for food – all rough occupations. Woman, true to Darwin, would not be muscular, but flexible to ease childbirth. Their more gentle handling of babies would be a biological necessity. Having children round her all day long she would develop a combination of firmness and kindness. Man would perhaps indulge in play, slightly roughly, and exemplify strength.

What I try to extract from this is that woman's firmness is her form of man's roughness, while her tenderness is her own. Man on the other hand teaches the reality of the world by his roughness; but he learns from woman that kindness to the children often pays. And he also learns that his sexual needs from woman are best facilitated by gentleness (there is a traditional idea that woman is roused by being knocked about; so far as this is not a myth, it would hold in limited degree only, not with the roughness of hunting).

So I am trying out a division of man as inherently rough with an acquired feminine gentleness; and of woman as inherently gentle with an acquired firmness (modified roughness).

Thus the idea adopted here is the idea that there is a recognizable inherent evolutionary difference between male and female of which man and woman contain ingredients from the other (but that man is not purely male in the sense originally described nor woman purely female).

With the subtle changes of societal developments the mixture has become extremely complicated.

But you have still only to hint to men (most men) that his femininity is prominent to upset his equanimity. On the other hand women (most women) are not disturbed by the corresponding charge. Which is in line with the point made earlier that man's femininity works against his maleness whereas woman's masculinity works in favour of her femininity. (Which would explain Bernard Shaw's belief that woman is the 'stronger' of the two sexes.)

Now the whole tenor of the above discussion hinges on interpersonal relationships. Freud's original theory was a one-body psychology, in which man recognized his maleness through possession of a penis and woman recognized her femaleness through 'loss of a penis'. Freud and the early analysts achieved striking results by this approach — from which I conclude that there are patients who suffer basically from a castration-complex; but it is also an open possibility that other patients suffer from some other source and are not specially disturbed by a castration-complex: in particular the root of their psycho-pathology may lie in being unable to adapt to the femininity (or masculinity) in their make-up.

I am not certain how far the early analysts did in fact introduce into their interpretations the idea of the castration-complex, or for that matter the idea of homosexuality. Their books and papers were full of these two ideas. But for one thing successful therapy may have ensued from other factors (notably listening and transference). For another, the early analysts seem to me to have been rather free and easy about the ideas. Thus their writings pounced on homosexuality, when I suspect they confused it with friendship and affection; they rashly perhaps relied a great deal on the intuitive insight and the boldness of the possibilities that opened up. Were these interpretations introduced into their discussions of their case-histories, or were they actually given to patients? In view of the general absence of explicitly stated interpretations and explicitly stated responses, we lack clinical evidence for these interpretations. For instance, it is common to come across the interpretation of homosexuality in connexion with prostitution, alcoholism, social life in pubs, physical fighting; but I have never seen the requisite evidence. Or take another case, the clergyman in cassocks, which might mean an effeminate component certainly but not necessarily more.

Thus it seems to me that the early interpretations of castration and homosexuality (anal eroticism) were possibly foisted on males — as one-body psychology — in mistake for a denial of femininity which can be expressed as a one-body psychology though it is basically two-bodied.[1]

In order to handle such a mixture of personality, I wish to try out the introduction of a new primary process (which I may have alluded to in other writings). This may be called the process of exchange of slices of personality. Like the basic primary processes discovered (invented?) and put to such profitable use by Freud (condensation, displacement, symbolization—including sub-limation—and secondary elaboration), this one is not available for observation. No television camera can pick it up. It is an interpretation, with all the usual difficulty of testing interpretations by their consequences. The presumption is that *personality-exchange* is a two-way traffic effected by the Kleinian mechanism of *projective-identification* and the Freudian mechanism of *introjective-identification*.

What I envisage is that personality-exchange is constantly taking place all through life. When a parent coos at a baby smiling or gurgling (or a cat purring) the suggestion is that something goes out to the baby ('That was a nice smile; I'm glad you feel pleased', or rather 'I'm gurgling in you') and something enters the parent ('That smile helps top me up') and even to a whimper the parent may convey 'I feel sore too', but also, 'My soreness does not damage me' (what Bion called accepting β-elements). Or sitting by the bedside when no words can help, or can be other than trite. In some discussion Thorner made a similar suggestion. Presence helps. Curiously enough my examples have to do with communication through silence—for if there is silence there is *ipso facto* 'presence'.

But these were not the experiences that suggested the idea. It originated in a game played on the beaches of Alexandria. Two people with a ping-pong bat each and a single tennis ball would hit the ball to and fro indefinitely until one of them missed. No attempt was made to hit the ball out of the reach of the other—on the contrary. No court was marked out on the sand. There was no scoring, no winning, no losing. Although I found this irritating because I wanted to read and the noise was disturbing, I was curious about the aim. And eventually it occurred to me that the two players were exchanging parts of themselves, that they were in fact *living*.

Another situation I was privileged to observe was of a toddler (alas I have no note of the age, but he was in nappies) in a large garden play-pen. A man quite well known to him stepped into the pen, whereupon the boy gave him a crust—nothing unusual about that. Almost at once the boy took it back—again a commonplace.

But then he gave the man the crust once more — and this is arresting. It would seem that it was not the crust that was important, nor even who possessed it. What mattered was the exchange: the boy gave something of *himself* (even if symbolized by the crust) to the man and received for himself something of the man.

Again at a cocktail party one is introduced to X, and one tries out something tentatively — the weather, the Government. This offer of oneself is found unacceptable, and one puts it back in one's pocket and tries out the latest novel. This produces animation, and X gives a good deal of himself in return. On this application of the supposed primary process, social life progresses, personalities grow (or are sometimes stunted).

If so, we are what those around us make us. Subject, perhaps, to the strength, flexibility, and outgoingness of our personality.

It seems possible that one's personality grows from the first suck to the grave, albeit, as its structure becomes more stable, it will alter less with the years (and with the well-known case of hardening of the [mental] arteries) a person will not develop at all after the age of perhaps fifty-eight, though maybe not after twenty-eight or twenty-two, if there is a lower limit at all. Fortunate the man who in old age deteriorates physically but whose mind continues to mature. Did I say to the grave? But it is a commonplace that often the surviving spouse takes on some of the ways and habits of the departed one.

Making a special application of the idea of personality-exchange to man and woman, to boy and girl, it is easy to see the toddlers (and crawlers) exchanging characteristics from the earliest days. It is difficult to measure the extent of the exchange. It is easy to see that two parents and siblings will be the most dominant factors involved. It is not easy to see precisely what factors produce strain in gender-identity — nor even why there should be such strain. One supposes that the physical propagation of the race places an emphasis on gender-identity. Going a step further, one might say that society itself is a by-product of gender-identity. Society, interacting with the biological gender, may create a *gender-brew* which turns out to be at odds with either society, biological gender, or both of these.

Can we make any attempt to see psycho-pathology as a product of the brew?

I think we could fairly say that schizophrenia is a disease in which practically all personality-exchange is lacking. Not quite all, however, since analysts and perhaps other schizophrenics have made some contact with a schizophrenic. The withdrawal in melancholia might be due to repudiation of the sex opposite to that of the gender-identity. Alcoholism might be seen as a desperate attempt to pretend to personality-exchange, i.e., an attempt to enter into personality-exchange, which would however be a pseudo-relationship. In obsessionality, what is denied is perhaps the gender-identity, a wish to have the opposite social gender-identity—to have a man's (woman's) mind in the biologically woman's (man's) body. This would differ in transsexualism in which the desire is to change both the body and the mind, and differ from transvestism in which (to take the male case) the masculine component is repudiated wholly, though presumably only temporarily; moreover the femininity would be required for the body only, not for the mind. For if a transvestite wanted to be female all the time, he would be a transsexualist. And this would hold even more definitely if he wanted to be female in mentality.

The homosexual may perhaps be presumed to have repudiated the opposite gender-component and to seek a partner of the same sex who shall also have repudiated the opposite gender-component. Concretely, a homosexual would seek the same constellation: he/she would have no other identification possible except through exchange of the only gender remaining to him/her. Moreover, this would possibly lay the emphasis on identification in many cases rather than on object-relationship, though object-relationship should certainty be possible.

Can we give a rough account of those I heard in the Middle East called 'bifocal'? One might suppose that, with a certain kind of split, a person might oscillate between acceptance and rejection of the non-biological gender. It may be noted that I have not distinguished 'active' and 'passive' homosexuality as this would render a brief sketch too complicated—indeed the whole application to the area of homosexuality would need a paper to itself.

I do not claim to know whether these constructions for the neuroses and homosexuality answer to actual experience. It should be stressed that all these applications are sketchy and involve a lot of guess-work. (I have come across very few homosexuals either clinically or in ordinary life.) I have sought only to give the merest indication of the kind of applications of gender-denial and personality-exchange that might be made by clinicians with appropriate experience of the field; I do not expect that all my guesses would survive, though I think some might.

The broad ideas of gender-denial and personality-exchange might throw light on one of the curious phenomena of our western society: the contempt and ostracism of homosexuality among males.[2]

And what about hysteria? The hysteric is *par excellence* one who cannot form fully genuine relations with others, strikingly those of the opposite sex though often they also have uneasy relations with the same sex. This is because of an insatiable desire to control the other. This means there is an internal war in which he (or she) cannot control his femininity (or masculinity) which is felt to threaten the natural gender.

We can even throw some light perhaps on that extraordinary phenomenon — cruelty. The newspapers, the news, the films set in the far past all bring home to us this widespread, so to speak 'natural', feature of human nature. But it is very hard to understand. What fun, what enjoyment, can one possibly get from watching barbarity? I would suggest that men practise cruelty to prove their machismo. That is to say, to demonstrate that they have no feminine weakness. So cruelty is denial of a man's femininity. Now of course women, some women though not so many, can be cruel. Catherine the Great was physically cruel in a man's way. For the most part, however, modern women's cruelty is more subtle, a mental goad. A man wanting to sleep with a certain woman may find he has seduced a hedgehog, though this would be rare. The cruel woman, it may be suggested, is also trying to prove her manhood and deny her femininity. Likewise sadism may be presumed to be one form, in the male, of denial of his femininity, which he has to destroy.

Could masochism be an introjected form of femininity that the male regards as an object of sadism?

These are but sketchy and tentative, almost casual, attempts to indicate how the process of personality-exchange might be seen to underlie various disorders. The hypothesis of this process would emphasize, not oppose, the importance of the work done by Melanie Klein, Margaret Mahler, and Eleanor Galenson on the significance of parental relations of subtle kinds in the earliest days of life, *especially* with the *father* brought into the picture. It might also enable a new type of interpretation to be introduced at all stages of analysis, whether of children or of adults.

From this point of view I would suppose that homosexuality is one (of several) possible extreme consequences of being unable to come to terms with the opposite sexual personality in oneself.

What I have tried to do in this paper is to depict man and woman in such a way that each contains a component of the other, and to view their differences as stemming from a social relationship between them, not excluding the castration-complex but avoiding postulating it as a universal and normal phenomenon. It would open up a whole new approach to psychopathology to attempt to derive the various neuroses from the conflict between the male and female trends. It might even be considered whether the perversions do not stem from an unfortunate admixture of the male and female characteristics.

Finally it should be added that the idea of androgynous blending is put forward as an underlay for other theories; it makes no claim whatever to provide a criterion of masculinity or femininity.

I will add a brief commentary on psycho-analytic writings, which from the beginning till recent times have, I think, confused, or at least fused, femininity in a man (Jung's 'anima'), with effeminateness, and homosexuality. It was implied all down the decades, though I have never seen it stated, that a man's friendship with another man was a (I think sublimated) form of homosexuality. If one looks through the early writings of the distinguished analysts for evidence of the homosexuality or homosexual component attributed to the patient under discussion, one finds *no evidence of homosexuality* but evidence of *femininity*. Now it is, of course, a proper hypothesis to try out that feminine traits spring from a homosexual tendency. But to assume it as a self-evident insight needs justification; nor do I know what such evidence would look like — one would expect perhaps that in fifteen-year-long analyses a fair number of interpretations of homosexuality would have been given and would have paid off, something that is highly questionable. Which suggests that it is in the writing up of a case-history that the interpretation enters the case-history, and this on the basis of hints which closer inspection reveals as femininity.

I shall leave on one side the question of effeminateness, which does seem a half-way house closer to, or a possible manifestation of, homosexuality. My main concern is with femininity.

Appendix: Some Relevant Literature

It is interesting to note that in recent decades, beginning perhaps in 1933, there has been a dim recognition of or implication that there is a difference. The ensuing glance at the literature may be so brief as to be found arid and can be skipped, but it is of interest in revealing how slow and slight was the change of attitude. I first note the attention given to the woman instead of exclusively to the man in Lewin (1933) and Rado (1933), but the first paper that seems to be noteworthy is one by Lampl de Groot (1933). She said:

> It is well recognized [was it?] that no man exists whose masculine traits are not accompanied by more or less obvious feminine characteristics, and likewise that there are no women who fail to show masculine tendencies (p. 489).

She attached little importance to the physical rudiments but held that the psychical traits confront all:

> This psychical struggle takes place in the development of every man and woman (p. 489).

It should be mentioned that the idea of the present paper, of a wholesale repression of one or other of the components, male or female, was suggested by Fliess to Freud, but Freud rejected it. Freud's contributions, though only partly relevant here, are so interesting, as is to be expected, that they should have a slightly more extended comment.

Freud's contributions are striking, perhaps more for what they do not tell us than for what they do. He said little about transvestism but wrote several times about homosexuality. Although his interest in this area goes back to 1905, perhaps his most illuminating paper on female sexuality was that of 1920, the one most referred to, despite his writings in 1931 and 1932. In that 1920 paper he showed himself incredibly well informed about the details of the field; he made no claim to understanding the condition, nor to being able to alter it by any kind of therapy. Perhaps the most interesting, and here the most relevant, point to emerge, is that the homosexual girl he had in analysis for a short while was in no way disturbed; she was not upset by her deviation and she displayed no signs of neurosis. Freud's remarks about a man's mind imprisoned in a woman's body (p. 170) have an extraordinarily contemporary ring about them—*plus ça change*. . . . It is especially noteworthy, in connexion with the disagreement between classical analysis and Melanie Klein, how Freud opened up the question and stressed the importance of *pre*-oedipal factors possibly before Melanie Klein, and sometimes even regarded the pre-oedipal as the more important for determining and explaining development. It is also noteworthy that, though Freud's discussion presupposed his conception of bisexuality, which the present paper does not fully accept in its classical form, he added a sentence in 1915: 'Thus the sexual object is a kind of reflection of the subject's own bisexual nature' (1905, p. 144). This the present paper does not accept: the present view is that man and woman have bisexual attitudes and psychical structure, whereas Freud held that they were physically bisexual. But he never seems to have fused transvestism with homosexuality. He refrains from any attempt to characterize the nature of man and woman.

The distinction I am concerned with seems recognized by Hendrick (1933), and is explicit in Bornstein (1935): dealing with the analysis of a boy he noted, ' . . . his wish to be not only a man but also a woman, in order to bear children like his mother'.

The distinction is clear also in Homburger (1935) and has to do with roles. Feeling female was noted by Wilson (1948). Of special interest is Freeman (1951) who dealt with the effect of pregnancy on breakdown in the male; and Evans (1951) on the same general area. Friedman and Gassel (1951) wrote on the mythology of birth from a male. Lewinski (1952) surprisingly fused homosexuality and femininity, but Plaut (1953) was concerned with both aspects of the personality. Bressler (1961) links testes and breasts, though it is not clear which view he supported. In attempting to examine the syndrome of obsessional neurosis, I (1964, 1966) attributed ambivalence towards the mother to a repudiation of femininity (without at that time having in mind anything like the present theory). Stoller (1964) seemed to lean in the direction of distinguishing homosexuality and femininity, and with him Greenson (1964), and definitely did so later (Stoller, 1968, 1975). Stoller (1965) also put forward the interesting thesis that *the male genitals have next to nothing to do with creating the sense of maleness.* Money (1970–71) distinguishes sex and gender, and attributes gender to a combination of biology and social factors. An excellent general account, in line with the most forward of these was given in Feinbloom (1976). And recently Limentani (1979), in a striking paper, has given close attention to gender-identity, and not allowed femininity in a male to be regarded automatically as homosexuality; he was also careful to separate castration-anxiety and the Oedipus complex. That is all I have come across. I may of course easily have overlooked significant contributions. But the citations given should suffice to show two distinct trends: the identification of femininity in a male with homosexuality; and a dim awareness that this is not so. I would also mention in excellent lecture given in Toronto by Ian Baker (1977), an analytical psychologist from Zürich.

In addition to the citations from the literature I will mention a fascinating occurrence that came to my notice. A little girl of $2\frac{1}{4}$ had a brother 17 months older. She asked why she couldn't pee standing up like her brother. I do not see this as penis-envy (far less homosexuality), though I do see envy of her brother. For those who regard anatomy as fundamental, and disregard social custom and the shape of our lavatories and chamber pots, it is worth pointing out that for the greater part of human history, and still today in many parts of the world, it is the custom for women to urinate standing up. It appears, therefore, that penis-envy, so far as it exists, cannot be purely inherent, but must be associated with some social practice.

Summary

The problem, to which this paper offers a contribution but no solution, is to determine what characterizes male and female. It is not solved by appealing to anatomy, and societal differences cannot be pinned down.

The approach adopted here is that both men and women have both male and female ingredients (which would have been acceptable before World War I to Adler and Jung; it approximates to Plato's Aristophanes), and 'androgynous' is used in this sense. What constitutes man and woman is regarded as societal. Those excellent researchers who study gender-identity do not tell us how to specify what a man is when he is part female. Following Darwin we seek an evolutionary difference, which would admit of the adoption of some of the other's characteristics. This leads to the hypothesis that a man's neurosis may be rooted in being unable to adapt to his femininity.

Conceivably, early analysts, who wrote freely of the *castration-complex* and homosexuality, did not often give these interpretation to their patients *in vivo*; and fused castration with femininity and fused homosexuality with friendship.

A new *primary process* is therefore suggested, consisting in personality-exchange; illustrations are given. It is used to explain how personalities may grow. If there is personality-exchange between a boy and his mother, one could view him as consisting of two sets of characteristics, m and f (analogous to x and y chromosomes). A crude attempt is made to interpret various neuroses in terms of a man's denial of his femininity; male homosexuality is interpreted as an extreme form of this. *Mutatis mutandis* for the female.

The approach implies that the castration-complex holds only for some men without being a normal process in all men. The rest might be explored as developing from a conflict between male and female trends.

Notes

1. Thirty years ago John Richman, in a discussion at the medical section of the British Psychological Society, questioned the suitability of a one-body psychology.
2. In some social groupings I have noticed that the men suspected homosexuals behind every door and were quick to try to nose out a homosexual. At Cambridge I recall a discussion of a newcomer of whom it was said, 'Yes, he looks it, but he isn't': so that the newcomer was given a certificate of being in the clear. Then in Egypt I recall the anxiety of the English overseas. On being put up for membership of a 'correct' club, my proposer actually asked me if I was one. I was astonished and told him, 'no', but reflected that if I had been I would presumably have lied. I would suggest that the horror of homosexuality entertained by the male is due to its prodding those elements of femininity in himself that he has not adjusted to.

14

The Psychical Self of Havelock Ellis

The good fortune has come my way to peruse the unparalleled biography of Havelock Ellis by Phyllis Grosskurth (1981). I had previously known little or nothing about him beyond what all the world knows, that he was the first in English to bring sex from the back streets to the drawing room. His biographer introduces us to his large circle—one gets the impression of a couple of dozen of intimate, very intimate, women friends. But it appears that none of these relationships was ever consummated. Grosskurth also concludes from the evidence that Ellis was impotent, and one of his intimates indicates that he suffered from ejaculatio praecox. There stand out Ellis's first great—perhaps his greatest—love, Olive Schreiner, then Edith Lees whom he married, and after her death, Francoise Cyon. Grosskurth, perhaps wisely, offers no explanation for his psychical love, which was not, however, as with medieval courtly love, totally asexual; for there were various intimacies short of intercourse. Still, it is regrettable that Grosskurth makes no foray into this, as she probably knows and understands Havelock Ellis better than anyone alive, or even dead.

Freud would offer us sublimation of, or perhaps displacement from, sororal incest. This seems at first sight unlikely in view of

Ellis's life-long encouragement of sexuality. Moreover, though the incest motif might have been a factor, it could hardly account for his restraint with *all* the women intimates; it would seem plausible that some would fall outside the incest barrier.

Not long ago I published (Wisdom, 1983) an alternative to Freud's theory of bisexuality. As I understand that theory, all men and all women, as well as being heterosexual, physically attracted to members of the opposite sex, also have an inherent potential varying from one to another for being physically attracted to members of the same sex. I have heard a fairly early classical analyst maintain that if a body of men were dumped, say at the North Pole, without any women, they would all display homosexuality. The alternative I put forward, for whatever reason, is that all human beings are 'androgynous', in the sense that all men — as indeed Jung held — have feminine components of *personality* as well as male and that all women have male components as well as female. I further suggested that certain phenomena could fairly easily be understood as a result of a person's being unable to come to terms with the secondary ingredient of the personality, and that in fact men have more difficulty in coming to terms with the element of femininity in their make-up than women have in accepting an element of maleness.

I do not propose to examine this idea further, but to enquire whether it could throw some light on Havelock Ellis.

Following on this hypothesis, it is natural to suppose that most men have, or have had, some difficulty in accepting their femininity, even if they surmounted it in early boyhood. It is not so easy to think of men as having difficulty in accepting their *masculinity*. Or rather, with such experience as we possess of psychopathology, we can see this difficulty arising in some degree. But there would seem to be a limit. Whereas one could envisage a man's totally repudiating his femininity (male chauvinist machismo?) it is more difficult to envisage a man's total repudiation of his masculinity.

Now this is what I conjecture happened with Havelock Ellis. (Or almost, for he appears to have had some masculine traits.) In these terms we can make sense of his impotence and his well-nigh exclusive preference for female friends — feeling, that is to say, a woman at ease among women. To this fact, however, must be added that his women were not 'just friends'; he practised sex with them in some form. On the present conjecture, Havelock Ellis could perhaps best be described as a lesbian.

This is all very well and might indeed be true, but to pass muster we have to enquire whether the feminine identification hypothesis may enable us to understand one of Ellis's astounding pieces of behaviour. He would get a woman intimate to urinate standing up in public in the most extraordinary places. I have found this pathological demand hard to interpret, but have come to the conclusion that the obvious one—of wanting to humiliate the woman—has possibilities. I do not attach importance to the places, since any public place would be extraordinary. What I suggest is that he wanted to display the women as one who was pretending to urinate more or less like a man, and therefore was not a genuine woman, and therefore was a lesbian. The purpose of this convoluted idea would be to see himself in her, i.e., to see himself as a woman making some claim to be a man.

Even if this account is tenable, the hypothesis still raises certain questions.

It raises a question about the women consorts. What did they want? Ellis's wife was in fact a lesbian. This is a historical fact. Most of the others were undemanding sexually, apparently content to be celibate. A few who were not, and found him lacking in vigour, moved on to another man. So those who put up with him would seem to have been lesbian-minded. At least this could be investigated. (Grosskurth could do it without much further research.)

Another, more difficult question, concerns what he did with his masculinity, in his unconscious.

Freud, if he were to agree with the present interpretation of lesbianism, would presumably say that Ellis's masculinity was repressed and sublimated. Unplausible as this may seem, it is not without some support.

Let us consider what signs Ellis showed of masculinity. He defied society over birth-control, about which he was a pioneer. His advocacy was not confined to learned journals but was intended to reach the market-place. He defied society in making sex a reputable subject; in this he was also a pioneer. These bold activities may be seen in sublimation terms as a manifestation of a masculine revolt against society. It is true that his revolt against society was probably socially rooted in that society's labeling him officially (i.e., on his birth certificate) as male and refusal to countenance his inner sense of being a woman (or if that is too strong, wishing he was one)—though it is also true that part of his advocacy of birth-control was on behalf of women. However all this may be, there is nothing odd or inconsistent in using masculinity in support of femininity. Ellis was also a considerable scholar (and scholarship in his day was confined to a male world). Thus sublimation is a serious possibility. It was one of Freud's most brilliant insights; and there is a certain plausibility about it in a simple case such as seeing gardening as a sublimation of nurturing children; the difficulty that faced Freud is still with us—to understand how the process of parturition and child-rearing can be transformed into another area which has nothing to do with children.

Alternatively—or additionally?—many today would see Ellis's masculinity as a split off component of his mind (personality or '*Seele*') in some projected form, seeking a home somewhere in his world as a projective identification. Perhaps a suitable location for it would be his revolt against society, his advocacy of contraception, in writing about sex and all its aspects, and in his devotion to scholarship and research.

This concludes my attempt to apply the idea of androgyny to Havelock Ellis and to interpret him as a lesbian, save to acknowledge that Grosskurth seems to have had the same idea or something like it much earlier. (Possibly the same diagnostic structure could be attributed to Akhenaten. One look at the colossi may convince.)

As an afterthought I can't help wondering, further, whether, if Havelock Ellis had been born, say seventy-five years later, he would have been transsexual and had the operations that can now be carried out to change his sex. My guess is that he would not have done so in his own day (though he might now) because he valued the then purely male world of scholarship and research.

Summary

An unparalleled biography of Havelock Ellis by Phyllis Grosskurth describes not only his opening up the subject of sex and pioneering contraception but goes in considerable detail into his warm intimate relations with a large number of women; these relations were never consummated; his wife was a lesbian.

Starting from my recent hypothesis of androgyny, the application is that while other men have had to come to terms with the femininity in their personality. Ellis could not accept his masculinity. Classical analysis might have thought him a latent homosexual; the present conjecture is that he was a 'lesbian'.

This hypothesis has to explain a very strange activity he went in for, to enquire what his women consorts wanted, and also to explain what became of the masculine strands in his nature.

References

Grosskurth, P. (1980). *Havelock Ellis*. London: Quartet, 1981.
Wisdom, J. O. (1983). Male and female. *Int. J. Psychoanal.*, 64:159–168.

15

The Diagnosis of Darwin's Illness

It is relevant to explain the inordinate delay in writing this review. Having read Colp's (a medical doctor) detailed, unbelievably detailed, catalogue of Darwin's illnesses, catalogue of diagnoses, rejection of virtually all these as inadequate, and his brief personal version of one of them, I came across two outstanding writings, one on Darwin's illness by Sir Peter Medawar (1967), the other more than adequate review of Colp's book by Prof. Bartley (1977). These two say just about everything there is to be said about the problem, its assessments, and the absence of an answer; so I was led to reflect on the *highly curious nature* of the problem of Darwin's illness and to form a new conjecture about its source.

Because Medawar's and Bartley's surveys are readily available, and because so many hypotheses have been shown to be inadequate, I need refer only in a very cursory way to the broad situation, the problem, and its proposed solutions. (I wish to thank Dr. Mauricio Kuperman for much help, and Dr. Hector Warnes and Dr. John Padel for comment on certain matters.)

This chapter was originally published as a review of Ralph Colp, Jr., M.D., *To Be an Invalid: The Illness of Charles Darwin*. Chicago, Ill.: University of Chicago Press, 1977.

First, it is of interest to read the immense list of Darwin's signs and symptoms (for which I am indebted to Colp's record based on Winslow's [1971] work, itself based on Clark): poor appetite (even loathing for food), nausea, vomiting, headaches, vertigo, faintness, cramps, clammy perspiration, epigastric pain, distension and fetid eructations, eruptions from skin and joints, convulsive affections, tic douloureux, paralysis, amaurosis, deafness, loss of sense of smell, loss of voice, spasmodic cough, asthma, palpitation. And more than these two dozen can be found.

Second, a brief word on treatments: Darwin consulted any number of doctors. He tried mercury, calomel, especially arsenic (which he took as people swallow aspirin), got the most relief (sometimes) from hydropathy, i.e., he wrapped himself in a cold wet sheet. Colp is candid about not knowing why Darwin sometimes got remissions while at other times the same treatments were unavailing. But this is a commonplace in both physical and psychological medicine.

Third, on diagnoses. Purely medical diagnoses have got nowhere. Arsenical poisoning was popular with some. Other suggestions were brucellosis, malaria, appendicitis, peptic ulcer, pyorroeha, gout. Medawar (along with some others) has given a measure of support to Chaga's disease, due to a bite from a bug when in Argentina, but this seems to have been ruled out. As this is the only plausible candidate from physical medicine, it would seem that there is no future in diagnoses from the field.

Bartley remarks that Freudians had a field day. He mentions three psychoanalysts (and there were others) who had no explanation in common; and indeed their diagnoses do not seem convincing or to have any real explanatory power. If the medical diagnoses do not get off the ground, and the psychological ones, though some have suggestive features, are thin, what are we to think?

Bartley is highly critical of Colp's foray into the field, at least as a piece of book making. He considers that the book amounts to a set of notes, is unreadable, and burdened with an apparatus of pseudo-scholarship. I agree with Bartley, and since I could not put the matter better—nor indeed nearly so well—I need make little further comment except to deplore the most inadequate index. As regards content Bartley rightly considers that Colp has done well in opening up a reconstruction of Darwin's emotional and intellectual situation. Moreover, as a medical doctor he has also done well to make it clear that no purely medical diagnosis is satisfactory. Colp's four pages of his personal psychological explanation centre on Darwin's feelings about his own theory of evolution (which the author acknowledges others had suggested before him). There is a force in this—as a subsidiary factor—for it led him to give up his deep religious beliefs. Bartley says this is worth pursuing and stresses that it was a very serious matter in early Victorian England. And Bartley rightly repudiates the psychological conjecture that Darwin's illness stemmed centrally from hatred of his father (who also had given up religion and was therefore not hostile to him, at least on this score), claiming that rejection of religion was more significant than hostility to his earthly father. This point had been even more explicitly put previously by Medawar who was developing a psycho-analytical explanation deriving from Kempf, Good, and Greenacre (Medawar, 1967, pp. 74–75, 78–79).

Granting that fear of the consequences of his evolutionary theory was significant—highly significant—all it provides us with is the trigger that brought on Darwin's attacks of illness. But I think it does do that, though of course we still need to know *how*, and *what*, it triggered off.

Let us remind ourselves that Darwin was a *chronic* invalid, for forty-one years from the time of his marriage, though he suffered before that too (indeed he was nearly too ill to go to his own wedding) from before the voyage of *The Beagle* onwards, though not chronically at that time. Despite this, he maintained a prodigious output of thought, research, and publication, and exhibited much physical energy. I shall return to the subjects of marriage and work, but now wish to add a theory, which is of a psycho-analytical type (Wisdom, 1983).

Instead of Freud's form of the theory of bisexuality, I have sought to bring into psycho-analysis Jung's theory of animus and anima, which are respectively the male component in the woman's personality and the female component in the man's. These may or may not be sexualized. The theory presented here continues that men (boys) have difficulty in coming to terms with their feminine aspects and that women (girls) have difficulty (less) in coming to terms with their masculinity. Otherwise put, they cannot bear the idea of being androgynous. (This theory is not to be confused with that of the castration-complex.) Various reactions to these (unconscious) troubles lead to the spectrum of psychological disorders and personality types. Of these, some plausible examples can be given, though it is far from clear to me how or whether the theory can be made to apply over the whole field or even over a great part of it. Suffice it to suggest as an illustration that the 'he-man', the pursuit of machismo, is possibly a denial that there is a female component in the male — the 'real' male — at all.

The application here is that Darwin's complaints were psychological and psychosomatic consequences of his struggle with such natural femininity as may have been his lot.

There is not very much evidence, but some pointers are interesting.

Darwin decried marriage, because it militated against work (work for him may be taken to be a male activity). He exemplified his attitude by nearly failing to be well enough for his marriage ceremony. Especially interesting are his reactions to Emma's (his wife's) pregnancies and confinements. His avowed reason was that she would not be in a position to look after him. But he was also most upset about her discomfort during gestation and particularly at parturition. He even said that her confinement 'knocked me up almost as much as it did Emma herself' (Colp, 1977, p. 27). (Americans may note that in English 'being knocked up' means only feeling very out of sorts.) Many psycho-analysts would see in his upsets at such times an *identification* with his wife (a projective identification). In other words his repudiated feminine component of personality was fastened in to her, as a means of getting rid of it yet satisfying it. He would not have seen this component, at other times, as being part of his creative personality.

Now there is, I think, another identification also — the unborn child or the post-partem child. He was evidently a devoted father. He would, then, contribute to his own welfare — of being looked after by his wife, which he complained of losing when she was pregnant, by identifying with the child. In line with this, we can see some of his signs and symptoms in terms of parturition and babyhood. Indeed some of these may be seen as manifestations of pseudocyesis.

I have not myself done research on the *Diary*. But it would be interesting to compare Darwin's first reactions to sons with those to daughters. One might hope to glean traces suggesting one kind of identification with sons as objects to be looked after and another kind with daughters indicative of the femininity he denied in himself.

Medawar, interestingly enough, though he thought the illness was primarily organic, also sought a psychological contributory constellation. He put forward in outline the Oedipus complex: he attributed many of Darwin's works to a strong concern with sex, for which he gave evidence and gave reason for connecting with Susannah (Darwin's mother) and Medawar held that for parricide Darwin substituted the abandonment of religion. One could add, on classical psycho-analytical lines, that, by his mother's death, when he was eight, he was likely to feel that she had desired him for his heavenly father.

In putting forward a different theory I do not imply rejection of Medawar's Freudian interpretation; indeed that complex may well be common to us all. But it does not explain much about Darwin's illness. And so far as it applies it may perhaps be rendered more intelligible by the theory of androgyny.

(I do not pretend that this is a well-worked out theory, nor to understand how it might account for all the mysteries of Darwin's illnesses, even though it seems to account for a number. I would recall, however, that Freud put forward a theory of the Oedipus complex, i.e., of incest with the mother plus parricide, and of the castration-complex, leading developmentally to the superego. He held that these factors, with auxiliaries in certain situations, explained several clinical types, such as hysteria and its varieties, obsessional neurosis, etc., though he never made it wholly clear how these factors did account for the consequences in question. However brash it may be to attempt to construct a theory on somewhat similar lines, it must be admitted that that is just what has been attempted above, even if with less convincing explanatory cogency than Freud was able to muster.)

References

Bartley III, W. W. (1977) 'What Was Wrong with Darwin', *The New York Review of Books*, **24**, 15 Sept., 34–36.

Medawar, Sir Peter B. (1967) 'Darwin's illness', in *The Art of the Soluble*. London, pp. 61–70.

Winslow, J. H. (1971) *Darwin's Victorian Malady: Evidence for Its Medically Induced Origin*, Amer. Philos. Soc. Philadelphia.

Wisdom, J. O. (1983) 'Male and Female', *Int. J. Psycho-Analysis*, **62**, in press.

16

Psychoanalysis Bypasses Homosexuality

Doubtless bisexuality was believed in by many in the psychiatric field before Freud, notably by Havelock Ellis, but apart from Ellis, Freud (1905) was the first influential figure to make it well known, and his *Three Essays on Bisexuality* constituted a watershed in the area of homosexuality. It was a seminal work though it contained no specific theory. It has been generally regarded by analysts as the basis of the subject and one gets the impression that most of them consider that somewhere along the line in that work Freud contributed vitally to the problem of homosexuality. This would seem to be a gross exaggeration, though he undoubtedly dropped a number of hints and suggestions that could be fruitful.

The most important idea of his work was that of bisexuality. Another was that homosexuality was always, at least in men, latent. He also considered that there exists a form of it which a person adopts because he or she cannot tolerate the idea of heterosexuality—in short a *defence*. Freud held that neurosis generally, and hysteria in particular, had an unconscious underlay of homosexuality. To interpolate a comment. It is reasonable to believe that there is (perhaps widespread) the latent form. But whether it is universal is another matter. About hysteria, it is likely that Freud's early patients, diagnosed as hysterics, had this defence. It is now a question whether there are any hysterics left. I have given a reason elsewhere (Wisdom, 1987) for thinking that the sexual revolution has made it socially impossible to have hysteria. This is not to say that hysteria is or was a socially induced disorder rather than a psychological one. It is to say that the psychological factors constituting hysteria could only make themselves manifest in a certain social setting. Apart from these forms of homosexuality, it has been generally held since Freud that there is a 'hard core' of the disorder which is unreachable by analysis. In any case there are almost no case histories of it and no cases of an analysis, even an unsuccessful one, of such a patient. It looks as though the analytic world had given up on the matter—a notable exception is McDaugall (1989). It is quite usual for analysts presented with what seems to be such a case to tell the troubled person, "I may not be able to cure you, but we may together reach a position where you will be able to live with your homosexuality." I do not think analysts should give up on the problem so easily. The reason for this attitude is not far to seek. For many decades the papers in analytic journals have been purely clinical, because of a misguided metascientific belief (see Wisdom, 1984) that the only way forward is by more clinical data. I have heard Anna Freud at one of her seminars say in summing up a presentation that "we need to know more about . . . " by which I understood her to mean more detailed clinical information. After 400 years of scientific development, the educated intellectual should know that the way forward has always been made by theoretical progress, by sometimes or often not very progressive forays that occasionally come off. I have made a theoretical attempt to tackle the problem of homosexuality (Wisdom, 1987). Whatever may come of my attempt, the main problem that needs to be tackled is Freud's claim for universality. It has first to be understood, contrary to the received opinion among analysts, that it will not be solved by adding up more and more cases, with or even without, the usual genuflection towards Freud.

Although I began with the assumption or bias that bisexuality was false, I could not nail it. On considering certain evidence put before me, which was impressive and new, I came to a different conclusion. There were two items, which I will outline.

One was anthropological evidence from a tribe in New Guinea (Stoller, 1985).

Stoller (1985), who is a psycho-analyst and psychiatrist, went to New Guinea with a social anthropologist. What they unearthed in a certain tribe was amazing. There was a standard upbringing for all males. Boys began in the company of women. Then at puberty they were suddenly transferred to the society of men. They were treated harshly but they had one social duty. This was to carry on fellatio with older adolescents. Being charged with semen was supposed to make the youngster martial, because the most important aim was to prepare for *defence*. But the seminal intake was also supposed to fit the youngster for marriage, reproduction being the next important aim. (Presumably in the order of priorities, it is no use preparing for the next generation unless you have made your tribe safe to reproduce in.) Half way through puberty, there was a sort of role reversal: the new batch of the younger ones replaced those providing fellatio and in their turn gave fellatio to a fresh batch of pubescents. This was (presumably) about the age of fifteen and a half. When marriageable, they were married off. Strikingly they never reverted to homosexuality again. It is regrettable that Stoller and his colleague had not found it possible to have done a parallel investigation of the female.

It would be impossible to understand what form of conditioning theory all this would fit: indeed it would be hard to fit into any theory, though Freud *might* have been equal to it. But this is not the point. The point is that the investigation provided a standard and socially accepted form of homosexuality. (I do not know whether the boys liked the business or just had to put up with it.) It is hard to believe that such a procedure could have existed unless upon a bisexual basis. Unfortunately we have no parallel in Western countries to compare it with. Perhaps if a social anthropologist were to investigate British public schools, we might learn something — but there of course sexual sublimation may take care of the sex-drive by concentration on games.

The second item is due to the work of a persevering neuropsychologist (Kempf, 1945, 1946). He is little known, but he did very careful work and used his mind skillfully. Unfortunately he wrote badly, so it is a distinct labour to read him. He was an orthodox

Darwinian. His idea was that all cells were bisexual. His detailed task was to show how the sex cells evolved and how the differentiation between male and female gonads developed. He appeared to have done a good job on this (not that I could follow all the detail). The author sees this in terms of ontogenesis and phylogenesis. So here we have another reason for considering homosexuality (the normality of which the author subscribes to) as normal. Still it would seem to me (if my opinion on such an abstract scientific level is worth reading) that a total sexual divergence into heterosexuality into irreducibly male, irreducibly female types would be compatible with the author's theory. It should be said, however, that the author's division of the gonads does not establish my point here. For the cells in the gonads of a male (and female) all are on the author's account, bisexual, which supports his theory and not my possible objection to it. It would be good if neurophysiologists were to take up this man's work.

So we have a strong argument from the structure of the New Guinea tribe, which favours bisexuality, and a rather strong though not conclusive argument from the work of Kempf (1945, 1946).[1]

I think it all adds up to the conclusion that (male) homosexuality, basically in the bisexual sense, is normal at some undetermined phase of human life (probably puberty).

In all the foregoing I have used the term "homosexuality" in the sense customary in such contexts to be restricted to *males*. Something more positive can be said about *female* homosexuality. I do not think Freud said anything significant about it, but Helene Deutsch (1947) did.

Having written at length on the structure of the female personality, setting out her belief that it consists of three basic ingredients, passivity, masochism, and narcissism, she tries to depict what constitutes the homosexual. She holds that it largely though not entirely springs from the mother-daughter relationship. If the daughter's masochism is excessive, and she is therefore subject to strong mother domination, she may react to the situation with increased masculinity. There may be an intermediate stage in which she flees to the father, but unless he is able, to improve her relationship with her mother, she will identify with him, and the outcome will be as before, increase of masculinity. Whichever way the girl develops she is on the path to homosexuality, assuming the reaction of masculinity to be very strong (a moderate amount of masculinity would simply produce the very common result of a rather masculine woman, so familiar to us all (women who have a life independent of their families need an element of this in their composition). In short, Deutsch treats homosexuality as having excessive masculinity, differing fundamentally only in degree. It is significant that on her theory, which is very convincing, homosexuality in the female is produced out of family relationships, and does *not* originate in penis-envy. Regrettably Deutsch does not distinguish, as has been done for men, a latent form, a form of defense, and a hard core. She does, however, seem to recognise the last form in a case report in which she was unable to resolve a feminine woman's homosexual fantasies, which had troubled the patient greatly.

It never seems to have been noted that with homosexuality in men the distinction between latent and the rest has been constantly drawn, but a parallel distinction among women has never been delineated. I have found nothing in the literature, including Deutsch, to nullify the distinction.

This completes my elaboration and outlining of most of Freud's theories from say 1882 to 1905. (But I will now cite the most significant of Freud's writings on the subject)

Freud on Homosexuality

It might seem that I had treated Freud's work on homosexuality too cursorily and demeaned it. In support of my somewhat low estimate of it, here are his main writings on the subject.

1. Written in 1925, published in German in 1927, is "Some Anatomical Differences between the sexes", English translation 1927, *Stand. Ed.*, 248–58. In his discussion of masculinity and femininity here, Freud reminds me of Helene Deutsch (to whom he refers) with his mention of narcissism (cf. 225, 229) though he does not handle the problem so effectively as Helene (255–56).

2. "Female Sexuality", *Stand. Ed.*, 21, 221–43. This contains a discursive account of masculinity in the female, the female's difficulty in overcoming her tie to her mother (226–27) – cf. Helene

Deutsch's theory again[2] noting that this can lead to masculinity or homosexuality (229–30).

3. *New Introductory Lectures on Psycho-Analysis, Stand. Ed.*, 22, lect. 33, 112–35. This writing is largely a discussion of masculinity and femininity in the female as a result of 'penis-envy' and 'the castration-complex'. But it also gives a brief account (130) of female homosexuality as a regression (13a), involving family relationships, to infantile sexuality.

4. In one of his greatest works, which he entitled *Three Essays on the Theory of Sexuality* (where he used the verb "to essay" in its older meaning of "to try"—and having a 'go' at it *was* what Freud was doing)—now known as *Three Theories on Sexuality, Stand. Ed.*, 7, 1905, re-inforced in subsequent editions. This work provides many stimulating ideas. But it is not about *three* theories. In fact there is in it no *theory* at all. It contains the famous saying that neuroses are "the negative of the perversions" (165) which Freud italicises; but this is an interesting corollary to be taken account of in a fully fledged theory—it does not itself amount to a theory.

Notes

1. I am indebted to Dr Cliford Scott for telling me about this work and lending me the book.
2. But we should remember that Helene may/must have got the rudiments of her ideas from Freud in her first personal analysis.

PART III

Women, Men, and Society

17

From Sex to Androgyne

The first thing that seems to strike many people about women and men today is that their ultimate is sex. This has to have a lot to do with the matter, of course. But less obvious, though available to the observant eye, at least an eye with a touch of social anthropology about it, is the future assurance of the group, the tribe, the society. From the point of view of phylogeny and ontogeny, the sexual apearatus, capacities, desires, and so on are more pawns in the process of ensuring the continuance of the social unit.

Immediately there crops up the institution of marriage. I must emphasize the extraordinary stress that has been placed on sex on all sides: the theatre, film, the Sunday newspapers of the yellow type. And, astonishingly at first sight, by various religions, e.g., the emphasis on sex in the marriage service, the virtually sole ground for divorce in the West till recent times. We should also notice the legal importance of consummation. The observer could be forgiven, therefore, it he concluded that sex was the most important thing in marriage, and indeed the most important thing in life.

Life in general has been much altered by the sexual revolution, so much so that it must be looked at anew. For the sexual revolution has produced a problem. Too many babies are born, some unwanted as illegitimate, some because divorce breaks up many homes, and some of them unwanted by their married parents. But there is, I think, an answer to all this. No, not restraint or contraceptives, or abortion, none of which works sufficiently well.

Marriage

To discuss woman and man, and enter upon the fringe of society, we cannot leave societal matters without some remarks on marriage, even though it is not explicitly mentioned in the ordinary run of psycho-analytic papers, despite being the subject matter of many analyses. Every community or tribe must have marriage laws or customs otherwise the group could not survive. Phylogyny and ontogeny required the continuance of the group of whatever kind it may be.

The continuance of the social unit depends on defence and on procreation. Defence is assured by the nature of man, and is part of the reason why man is given pride of place over woman, for without defence there can be no secure procreation.

Marriage in Western culture tends to be widely mislocated on sex. The social emphasis comes in many ways. The churches make a big point of it in the marriage service. The law bears on it, in that before 1969, virtually the sole ground for divorce in Great Britain was sexual infidelity or nullity where the marriage was not sexually consumated. Societally, if a marriage breaks down isn't the finger usually pointed at sex, though it is sometimes pointed at drink or gambling?

If sex isn't the most fundamental item in marriage, what is? No one knows. I have noted some half-dozen other important factors that make up marriage as well as sex. But there is nothing to indicate that sex is the most important of them — and nothing in all of them to show that marriage is for life. The embedded proposition, is *synthetic a priori*, and would have defied even Kant to prove it.

The unpalatable result of our enquiry is that societies as we know them have not begun to understand their societal basis.

Phylogyny and ontogeny have produced an extraordinary species, homo sapiens, which has inhabited the Earth for perhaps a hundred thousand years. This animal has shown a potential for understanding a few things. But it also seems to want to avoid understanding and, indeed, to wallow in ignorance.

Homo sapiens has perhaps two attainments to its credit. The only thing many has been adept at is fighting, though usually not very good at it. The other attainment is the discovery of language, at which he has been very ingenious (Hattiangadi, 1987).

I think now is the time to make a new proposal for the regulation/irregulation of sex/marriage. The proposal I would make is this. Sociologists would be able to find the approximate number of years at which marriages tend to become stable, i.e., not followed by desertion, separation, divorce, etc. Let us call this marriage year Q.

My proposal is that men and women should be encouraged to live together as they wish, with a hopeful commitment, but that it would be *illegal* for them to have a child before the par year. After that they could bring up their families in the belief that they knew what marriage was like, and that they would continue to be the parents of the children born after Q. (There could be certain exceptions due to age).

Naturally the chief Western religions would not welcome the idea — and I cannot think of a suitable inducement. To the state it would mean less money doled out for illegitimate children having only one parent. No country is likely to be enthralled by the idea. But let it be remembered that Great Britain, or England rather, has a long history of social reform from 1215, weakening the power of the King, to the bill of rights, the reform bills, votes for women, improvement of right to divorce, and recognition of freedom for homosexuals. Indeed, the only major reforms left for Great Britáin to introduce are euthanasia and a bar to birth before Q.

We turn now to specify in more detail what is involved in androgyny.

The broad idea may be attributed to Aristophanes, or to Jung or to a new view I have put upon it. It is namely, that man (most adult men) contains a female component in his personality whether consciously or not, and parallelwise that woman (most adult women) whether consciously or not contains a streak of masculinity in her make-up. 'Masculine' is here taken to mean 'active' as it usually is in writings on the subject and 'feminine' to mean 'passive' — however unsatisfactorily — but has no reference to sexual behaviour.

Androgyny is a psychological concept. Whether it presupposes bisexuality or not I do not here enquire. But some biological springs it must have. It is not to be assumed that feminine men or feminine women or any other combination are born such. Hormones and heredity plus random genetic changes could underlie numerous, a dozen or more, tendencies, which will then be subject to parental, not to mention sibling and other social influences. This is so whether the roots just mentioned are regarded as 'instincts' as Freud and others postulated or multiple instincts as other psychologists have tried instead, or an unspecified assortment of biological roots, which is where I prefer to leave the matter. By a feminine man, for example, I mean one in Western culture whose biological roots give rise to a mind involving factors that either prenatal or postpartem have become conjoined sufficiently to form a personality; which however may be malleable enough to undergo psychological or social change, including change through psycho-analysis and admitting of growth with personal experience. In what follows I will be considering more or less stable types of adult women and men in the West.

A theory of this sort would be anathema to most men as an insult to their masculinity. A few women might also be expected to object. But I think that many women, while disagreeing with the theory and the rough definitions, might look on it as possible, certainly not derogatory, and some might even be proud to have a strain of masculinity in their nature.

Whatever view adult men and women might make of it, I put it forward as a hypothesis to see if it will throw any light on the age-old question of the nature of men and women in society. In my opinion androgyny can shed light where Freud's idea of bisexuality did not. We may need both theories. They are possibly not incompatible, but maybe androgyny has totally different biological roots. In the present work, however, it will suffice to concentrate on androgyny alone.

A former professor of experimental psychiatry (Freund, 1983) at the University of Toronto — I was fortunate enough to have two interviews with him — told me that he had a method of diagnosing homosexuality in the male. He did not, unfortunately, distinguish the more gentle 'feminine' type, which he seems to have had mainly in mind from the rougher extremely macho type. I will refer to them as the f-type and the m-type adult. But there is no intention here of denying that there exists a huge range among men from ultra-macho to strong to gentle to ultra-gentle with thin bony structure, all capable of performing the sex act. Nor of denying a similar huge range among women. I am inclined to think, however, that no male can be so ultra-macho as to have no component of femininity *at all*.

This psychiatrist, moreover, also had means of measuring femininity in men of a scale from 1 to 10. Further, that homosexuals had a rather high ranking on femininity. I suppose, but did not get it confirmed (or rejected) that a low femininity score was compatible with normal heterosexual activity. If this is so, then it would agree with my hypothesis that a degree of femininity would be normal in the ordinary run of heterosexual men of heterosexual bent. But this tells us nothing about the m-type.

All this, alas, leaves out women. This is partly because the above psychiatrist deals only with men, either because they refer themselves or because they are referred by the courts.

This did not, however, prevent him from giving me a few well-informed opinions. All my first interview he agreed with the Masters and Johnson figure of 5 percent for homosexual males. This incredibly high figure means that one in twenty of all the men you have ever met were homosexual. At my second interview a few years later I asked whether he still held to the figure. He said he would now put it at 3 percent for men and for women a bit lower.

Obviously there is much obscurity here. These figures give us no breakdown into 'hard core' homosexuals, those who have had some episodes, and latent homosexuals. But they highlight a problem area.

The idea of androgyny would be easy to apply to patients, whether in psychotherapy or in psycho-analysis. But we can first sift out the old question of the nature of women and of men by considering some new hypotheses and not leave it so entirely in the dark as Freud did when he admitted defeat.

Andogyny Elaborated

The idea that destiny is determined by anatomy has worn thin. It is not being denied that a man has some propensity for having sexual relations with other men; but it is averred that man has a feminine streak in his personality. This would seem to hold generally (though I do not know how to look for evidence).

It is a factor found intolerable by men in most countries; up to the recent past in Great Britain, still intolerable in America, and I think in South America. Any suggestion of femininity will get under a man's skin. It is taken to be bordering on an accusation of homosexuality. But it is not the same thing at all. The feminine component of personality can be, in these days, measurable. It does turn out, however, that too much of it may lead to homosexuality. But excess is one thing; a reasonable amount is quite another.

It is similar, though not quite the same, mutatis mutandis, with women. For a woman to have a male streak in her personality does not imply homosexuality. Nor does the idea of a degree of masculinity in her composition usually worry her consciously.

Turning to androgyny in men: While men are often ashamed of their femininity, women on the other hand are often proud of their masculinity. (And men sometimes are too, if their consorts have some masculine qualities.)

It has occurred to me that many social difficulties which men suffer from are due to their being unable to accept their own femininity — and to a lesser extent the same obstacle, though smaller, confronts women. I have called this mixture, whether in men or women, *androgyny*. The hypothesis of androgyny, which I would regard as more important than bisexuality, is that difficulties arise when the mixture is inappropriate.

Man is constantly trying to establish his masculinity. This may be attempted by repudiating all femininity in his nature, and hence, for example, putting enormous emphasis on things macho. For which there can be a huge range of variants, from in some cases politicians strutting about, to young men making a display at a party, from lack of decorum on the centre court at Wimbledon, to riding up and down on a loud motor-bicycle, from bull fighting to Star Wars.

Women, likewise, are generally on the look-out for ways of increasing femininity, e.g., in fashions and decoration. To emphasize the difference with Freud's theory of bisexuality: his was almost completely a physiological theory; perhaps it was psychophysical or psychophysiological; the present idea of androgyny is psychological, concerned with components of personality. But it does not exclude bisexuality.

This hypothesis has value for man. It gives a comprehensible way by which men and women can begin to understand one another. By projecting his feminine feelings into a woman (i.e., by seeing feminine parts of himself included in her) he can begin to understand what he finds there. By associating with her he can enrich the feminine part of his own personality by taking into himself part of her nature (there are psychological technical words for this, of course, but I think anyone can understand what is meant in straightforward English). Curiously enough, the possibility is open that, by his embodying more femininity from the world of women, a man may end up with increased masculinity — a consummation so devoutly to be wished, that many men will go to all lengths (except the one mentioned here) to avoid it.

Thus a marked difference between men and women is that men are ashamed of their femininity, feeling it detracts from their masculinity; while women do not, to anything like the same extent, reject their masculinity, but accept it without feeling that it damages their femininity. We can understand that a man fears (as Stoller (1974) would put it) being drawn back into his original oneness with his mother. A woman need not fear this. Moreover, she can indulge an outgoingness towards her father, pleasurably and without risk. On the other hand there isn't all that much about his father to attract the boy; indeed he may sense in his father a disagreeable kind of touchiness, a sense that things must be done according to a certain drill. A father is unlikely to bother to ensure a girl's doing things in a similar routine, even if he understands what it is.

It would seem then that a man needs in his consort a reflexion of his femininity. Then he need not worry about it. It is active in and through her. And similarly for her. The composition depicted here provides structures by which they can at least in part understand one another. But there can be misunderstandings. Thus when a simpering Victorian female gets grappling hooks into a man, he may not realise till much later that she has a considerable masculine component that she will not satisfy in and through him, or in some direct way (such as mending fuses), and that he may not be allowed his masculinity.

This lack of meeting ground between men and women may perhaps be explored by means of an idea I have put forward in another field.

The idea is that groups of all kinds are divided from one another by their weltanaschauungen, their overall ways of seeing themselves and their world. For example, biologists have been divided according to whether they saw man as an evolutionary product from the ape, the fish, and the cell, or alternatively as a separate creation. This scenario is of men for the battlefield, women for the home, childhood, and nursery. Those who subscribe to these two weltanschauugen can scarcely discuss basic questions with one another. Again, the Ptolemaic weltanschauung places man firmly at the centre of the universe. We know that it was a matter of life and death for those who followed in the footsteps of Kepler and Galileo after placing the Sun at the centre. In our own day the Big Bang weltanschauung has been opposed by that of the Spontaneous Creation and Disappearance of Matter. Freud's way of seeing man has been strongly opposed by the weltanschauung of Conditioned Reflexes. It is even more interesting when one looks at some of the approaches that have been totally lost and been discarded and forgotten such as two-fluid frameworks for electricity or heat. As a working hypothesis let us suppose that such opposing weltanschauungen have divided men more intensely and more irreparably (Muslim and Hindu, Irish Unionist and Catholic, Jew and Arab) than have any empirical scientific theories. The fierce oppositions from history suggest that it is particularly difficult to penetrate an opposing weltanschauung.

Making use of this approach, I suspect that women have a very different weltanschauung from men. Whether this is wholly true or only in part, even if they have part of their circle of approach in common, it would surely be a worthwhile enterprise to enquire into the weltanschauung of women. The initial idea is that women's weltanschauung (also men's) lies in their various boundaries between their feminine and masculine components of personality. They want these boundaries understood (though not understood so well that a man can gain control over them). It is difficult for a man to understand the boundary since he has trouble about accepting his own boundary until he recognises his own femininity.

Can we arrive at anything about a woman's conception of her own femininity? For too long the male idea has centred on frilly lace and getting all gooey over babies. The latter probably is a genuine part of a woman's femininity. But it is not far removed from a man's femininity (though he has it under control, so far that it almost ceases to exist, though he will display it over a dog) and there is nothing shameful about his allowing it to blossom. Women, too, take an overt interest in personal relations, which is one reason for hoping for improvement when they take over world politics. Men's conception of personal relations stresses too much the handling of people in terms of Machiavellian consequences or of case-records. A woman is more likely to try to satisfy another's needs, and let the consequences be handled in due course whatever way the dice fall. This is no more than another instance of her innerness. There is of course, a pragmatic difficulty here (it is possibly because its being a country ruled by pragmatic philosophy that America is more male dominated — on the surface — than many other countries). For operating in terms of personal relations and needs, which violates the legal idea of constancy and standard procedure, this inviolable constancy can obviously go too far. It is at this point that women may need to take account of whatever maleness they possess.

The arts have long been regarded as the province of women. It was a bit 'soft', verging on effeminacy, for men to be too interested in the arts. There may be a grain of truth in this. For if homosexual men tend to have an overdose of femininity, this would lend sense to the curious fact (as often claimed) there is a high proportion of homosexual men in the fields of the arts. But a large endowment of femininity would make sense of the fact that nearly all the great painters, musicians, and poets (except Sappho) were men.[1] Not, however, the English novelists. The women novelists were in a position to put their grasp of personal relations to direct use.

Women are more gifted than men at assessing personality. This quality should put women at the forefront of all sorts of activities, from novels and plays to running businesses, to being psychological advisers, to political activities, to doctoring. How they would affect the law I have no idea. A study of policewomen should teach us something. Possibly the invention of the institution of the ombudsman, invented in Scandinavia, is a manifestation of femininity's trying to soften man-made justice.

Where are we, then, with woman's weltanschauung? We have noticed several differences between the sexes, which play into the dichotomy of the toughness-warrior axis versus the nest-building and nurturing axis. But there are also certain other feminine characteristics, greater sensitivity to culture, the need to be valued (not just as cooks, etc.) — the need to influence without resort to wile, the wish to strengthen a man's masculinity not by encouraging his machismo but by understanding his femininity — while having her frilly lace if she wants it — an interest in opening a man's eyes to the arts, the need to recognise that men have a genuine problem over the legalistic and economic side of life.

Note

1. It is possible that all creative men have a high degree of femininity.

18

Women

Assuming androgyny, we can tackle the problem of womankind head-on, from scratch. My friend Dr. Michael Fordham (1989) has remarked to me on a certain *innerness* about women. In other, or I hope suitably expanded words, women live much more of their lives inside themselves (despite outgoingness towards other people), which I suspect means that they have an untouchable core to be manifested in part only on very rare occasions. It seems to me likely that part of this innerness lies in the willingness to tap their component of masculinity. And that another part, which would traditionally be seen rather as freedom from the more finicky forms of male moral values.

It might be suspected that the widely feared female secretions — not only among primitive tribes — would be supposed to draw their power from the core of innerness. Be that as it may, the power of the woman would seem to lie in the ease with which she can utilise her inner core or shut it off. Which in its turn would determine her access to her masculine components of character. And her weltanschauung would be an uncompromising refusal of access to it mainly by the male.

If this hypothesis is anywhere near the truth, do any testable consequences flow from it? One would be that at times women would be highly intractible; some item or other would not be negotiable. Moreover, if by some means a woman was forced to act against her inner nature, one might expect her hormone system to be in disarray, not to mention its resulting in a severe psychological disorder. A further consequence that might be anticipated would be the fear of the drying up of their bodily secretions (explicit among some primitives). Of this fear there could be a variety of manifestations, from being frigid to fear of being unable to conceive, to fear of uncalculated pregnancy, accompanied by food-fads to counteract. A further consequence that might ensue would be much increased activity aimed at boring into other people's lives, both men and women: this would have the defensive aim of security, by finding the other people unharmed by that curiosity, or even being comforted by other people's having afflictions. A more personal outcome would be the absence of fear of fragmentation of their core, free of the anxiety of having no control over their lives.

What, then, is central in all this? Innerness, meaning the capacity to live their lives to a large extent within themselves — without being 'withdrawn'. This form of what one might call remoteness could induce anxiety in a male because he would not know what was going on, and it would suggest that there was something he could have no control over. The various other factors alluded to — the strange substances in the female body, apparently inexhaustible, and apparently infinitely demanding — might well appear to be the manifestation of an inner highly powerful core. Freud would have been right in seeing a core of this nature as essentially libidinal. But he might have been wise to listen to the wider version of Jung's, and indeed to Adler's, notion of need for power, as being a component. It could still be argued that of these the most basic was the libidinal one. But when one has a blend, does it remain any longer a matter of any significance which component dominates the brew? Putting this still more briefly, the innerness of woman is a non-negotiable core, consisting at a minimum of a constellation of secretions, of which we may be allowed a glimpse, but subject to the absolute restriction — Thou shalt not touch the key.

A rough summary would be that woman wants man to understand: to understand her inner workings quite well — but not too well.

Femininity

At the cost of repetition I wish to insist on retaining the idea of femininity. It is a good word and stands for all that is most lovable in the female. There is no need to confuse it with the old view of women, which confined it to looking after babies, cooking, and tending to her man's wants. She can also be good looking, have her own ideas, seek attainment, be charming, witty, warm, intelligent, with a will of her own, lively, serious, a good listener, a good talker, helpful physically as well as mentally, efficient, be a reader, a gardener, entertainer, sociable, motherly, helpful, adviser, tactful. I do not say how many of these qualities a woman should have to count as feminine. The fainting, simpering, generally complaining Victorian-Edwardian caricature is no longer part of the idea of femininity.

From this distinction, I turn to Helene Deutsch's assumptions about the basic characteristics of a woman. These are passivity, narcissism, and masochism. She regards the proper balance of these as essential. Too much masochism is likely to lead to homosexuality or over-strong masculinity. Too much narcissism may spoil her object-relationships. Too great passivity may lead to any kind of reaction. A woman needs a good charge of narcissism, even though through its excesses narcissism has got rather a bad name. She needs a minimum of masochism to fulfill many of her roles in normal life, since some degree of pain is usually her lot. Passivity is needed to fit in with many of her social roles. Of course, Deutsch is unable to say how much of each component is required. She had to be guided by what she found in patients in analysis, and by what she learned from interviews with psychiatric patients. In short she could recognise adequacy intuitively. Since passivity is not likely to be in short supply, I think that what normality boils down to is a good supply of narcissism to keep control of masochism.

I will add here an idea that struck me recently. It is in two parts. First, woman are 'governed' by what I would venture to call—if philosophers are not listening—the "philosophy of blood". After their first decade they have their menstruation. I understand that in Wales this is known as the "bleeding". Then anytime towards the end of the second decade or later, with varying degrees of pain, comes the rupture of the hymen, which often or usually, though not always, brings pain with bleeding. Thirdly comes childbirth with bleeding, and usually pain. Finally there is the menopause. Though this refers to the cessation of the periods, there is some-times some pain and bleeding. These well-known facts are virtually never put together, not even by Deutsch, though I found enough in her books to put them together as the 'philosophy of blood'. I propounded this first at a graduate seminar at York University, Toronto, in October 1988. One of the women present mentioned that this had been remarked on by a woman writer. The reason for the silence about it in the psychiatric literature, especially psycho-analysis, is that all women know all about it and have little or no reason to mention it. And men would regard the subject with distaste and ignorance, and not think it suitable for discussion, virtually unmentionable.

The second part of 'my' thesis, since I can scarcely call the first part mine, is to apply Melanie Klein's theory of the male envy of the female. The application is very simple. Since man cannot emu-late woman's philosophy of blood by 'natural' means, he can have recourse to regular bleeding by killing, murder, and war—which have for so long been men's preoccupation.

I wish to bracket the philosophy of blood with what I said earlier about male and female. The woman who accepts the feminine component of her personality has to come to terms with the bleed-ing. It may be that the bleeding affects her personality or it may be the other way round, i.e., that her acceptance of herself as a woman might affect her troubles in the four phases of the philoso-phy of blood. I am inclined to guess that the former is the correct order.

Returning to the feminine graces, we have reached the conclusion that femininity lies mostly in having enough masochism for the woman's lot while having a goodly supply of narcissism to keep the masochism under control, and therefore enough narcissism when bleeding requires it, so that her narcissism sees that her bleeding is after all, the best of herself. The hard core would resist either masochism's or narcissism's being pushed too far.

To draw a few threads together. I think the 'philosophy of blood', explains, or constitutes, the hard core. It obviously explains many facts hitherto included under the umbrella of anatomy, and a great deal of women's social behavior, such as putting men in charge of business and the big outer world, having a different weltanschauung from men, and even the wish to become emancipated—to be as men, to be freed from the 'philosophy of blood' itself—to be freed from themselves.

In other words I see women as caught up in an eternal struggle whether to become feminine or not to become women.

19

Men

It has been wisely pointed out to me by my friend Dr. Clifford Scott that, if writing about women, something should be said about men.

There is a myth widespread among women that a man wants a woman for just one thing—sex. And that may be all *some* want. But man's wants of course are as complicated as woman's. As they see themselves, men want excitement, sport, and the clang of battle—disillusionment with war is recent. By and large I would suppose men have always wanted the same sorts of things as women want: companionship and understanding, reliability, ability to cope, a social understanding of other generations, generosity of outlook, charitability, sternness, gaiety.

As portrayed above, it seems to have emerged that for some reason men have to have a bisexuality phase, with a probability that some homosexuality is normal during adolescence.

Women likewise have to be bisexual, though for totally different reasons. The main one is that women can never totally discard their first libidinal ties to their mother. This is most clearly stated by Stoller (1974), though if well adjusted to her mother, the little girl can develop in the femininity direction. There are also family influences as depicted by Helene Deutsch.

The boy has to detach himself from what used to be called tellingly the mother's apron strings. The boy has a harder time of it than the girl.

Both sexes have to accept their feminine component. There can be little doubt that above all others, what a man wants from a woman is belief in, and support for, his masculinity. This may come in a variety of shapes, such as being at his beck and call, pride in his performances, or absorbing his feminine traits. His masculinity has to be assured — and reassured. His femininity has to be, insofar as it is recognised, put to the service of some masculine virtue — petting the baby will assure him through the mother that the little boy will grow into a fine chap like his father.

The point can be put more strongly. Because she is, as Bernard Shaw pointed out, the stronger sex, it is necessary that a woman can handle her man's most acute troubles. It may be by conveying a suggestion as to how he can get out of some difficulty, but in such a way that he is not fully aware of what she is doing — ideally that he believes he thought of the freeing idea himself; or better that he does not need to lean totally on her suggestion. Going one step further back in such matters, he would value deeply from her a warning light before he makes a 'cock-up'. In short, guidance (in a non-moral sense).

So far we have noticed that what a man wants from a woman is support for his masculinity, and in a different way support for his femininity. Then guidance. That means guidance in a man's world, for which task the woman will need both her masculinity and her femininity, if she is to hold the reins.

In one particular case, however, she is to exercise caution. She must put her narcissism to *his* use. Hence not only does her narcissism have the function of controlling her masochism but some self-admiration could be used to boost his masculinity which could become, by her admiration of him, replaced by her narcissism whatever form she finds, physical, social, or any other.

I think Freud was right. There is such a thing as 'primary' narcissism for males as well as for women — at least in the sense I have tried to give it earlier — the upholding of a person's place in the world. A woman has to use the man's narcissism wisely.

A woman can help a man to accept defeat without injury to his male or female components — probably already included in what has already been said.

Just as a woman has an untouchable core, so has a man a core in his male-female androgyny which he cannot allow to be stretched without his disintegrating as a personality. This may of course be taken to be an elaboration of his narcissism.

On inspection it seems clear that the significant points here are essentially group-dependent. I cannot see a man's or a woman's having narcissism without its being attributed to the one or the other by a group. The point hardly needs to be made à propos of guidance. I suppose one could conceive of a world wherein men emphasized their machismo simply for the edification and approval of other men. (Björn Borg gave up being a world champion).

In this connection, while women live inside themselves and want to be just themselves, a woman, too, as with men, is but a woman among women and is subject to being constituted by womankind. So we cannot escape from groups. But all this will have to be deferred. Just as matter, according to Einstein, is a knot in space-time, so one might say that men (and women) are knots in an ether of similar knots.

We can get some further clues about masculinity from social anthropologists about primitive tribes and societies.

It has long been known that during menstruation or childbirth women were secluded in a menstrual hut away from all contact with men. The men fear menstrual blood and vaginal secretions — in effect the insides of the woman's body, the inside contents being highly dangerous. Dangerous to what? The answer that suggests itself immediately is 'masculinity'. It comes over loud and clear that the man will be undermined as a warrior if he is drained of his semen. We know of course how for centuries and millennia manhood depended on his skill in and love of fighting. On the other count, although the other main function of the warrior was to perpetuate his kind, he clearly did (see Stoller, 1985) fear exhaustion by the insatiable demands of his wife. This fear is eked out by a curious form of ignorance. (At one time it was thought that primitives did not know of the connection between intercourse and childbirth. This must have been a fairly complicated discovery, without the aid of statistics. For, although a swollen belly would often appear a few months after coitus, there would also have been many cases in which pregnancy did not follow. "Why sometimes, why not other times?" must have been a perplexing question. However, it was concluded by anthropologists and psycho-analysts that primitives had far more knowledge of the realities than had at first been thought). In the present context, there seems to be no doubt that primitives, at some stage at least, do not know that the man manufactures his own semen, but thinks he suffers from a shortage, and this is fraught with social consequences. The young adolescent has to gain his supply, by fellatio, from older adolescents. Stoller has not (yet) explained where the initial supply first came from. But given the older adolescent's 'knowledge' of his limited store, he has two worries to face. One is not to lose too much semen when going through the ritual of starting the younger adolescents on the road to manhood (See chap. 16). The second is, when a youngster has completed his adolescence and becomes married, not to be drained by an insatiable wife. Despite the man's belief that he does not manufacture semen, he has no corresponding doubt about the women's capacity to make surplus blood or vaginal secretions.

Here we are perhaps on the track of why man looks on woman as the stronger animal—she is productive, he is not. He has possibly never got over the humiliating deficiency, that she can grow a baby in her belly, whereas he cannot, and perhaps his non-functioning nipples are analogous to the flaps over non-pockets a cheap tailor may put on a ready-made jacket.

Man has of course certain unique possessions. He has a penis. Woman does not. But, I would conjecture, he does not really believe it and suspects that she does have a penis—but inside, perhaps in the vulva (and clinical cases of this belief are known [Scott, personal communication]). If this is the belief, it would have to be accompanied by the idea that the female penis has no access to semen to ejaculate.

The man though he possesses a penis, cannot, he imagines, supply it with semen at will; he has to work hard to gain a store of semen, and he is afraid of its running out. I have not found why a woman's inner discharges are so dangerous. But I would suppose that it is because of being sexually arousing. This is obvious for vaginal secretions; and the menses are widely regarded in the same light — whether the man is aroused then, or the woman is more seductive then, makes no difference. If the man is drained — and let us remember that intercourse is widely forbidden on the night before a battle — he will be crippled as a warrior and useless for siring.

There must, I think, be some connection in men's minds, if we could only find it, between the property of semen to fertilise and what is required to make a man into a warrior. It is worth considering whether rape connects the two. For raping, as well as being obviously (perhaps too obviously) sexual, also displays assault and mastery even culminating in the death of the victim. And possibly the horror of rape displayed by women stems from their being unwillingly treated, in part, as a warrior — as a man. (Though I suspect that in many cases rape may not be practised for sexual satisfaction at all, only for power over the woman).

There is an interesting society in which a young man had to establish his manhood by taking part in attacking a neighboring group, and returning successfully with a head. As it was in a British colony, and the British are notoriously squeamish about such customs, they put a stop to it. When there was a revolt, the British, ingeniously enough, persuaded the natives to go after wild boar instead of other humans (a substitution that could have come straight out of Freud's book, though it is not here suggested that the Colonial Office read up their Freud). It seems to me that in their order of priorities, those natives had to prove themselves warriors first, before they could have sex. Thus the element of toughness came before procreation. And to this day there is a widespread idea that a man should be a bit rough on his woman. There seems to be a widespread idea that a man cannot be potent unless he is tough.

It begins to look as though the early Freud-Adler dichotomy should have been a partnership. (As it was, Freud set the stage for the All-American Hollywood male in a bedroom setting, while Adler endorsed, in effect, the Prussia of Clausewitz and Bismarck).

We should, however, look back at the custom reported above by Stoller. The young pubescent, forcefully segregated from his mother and all other women, is locked into a purely male society. Harsh treatment by the adults is presumably aimed at hardening the youngster for his future role as a warrior. This is not, perhaps very surprising. More important, I think, from a societal point of view is that the young pubescent in New Guinea has to fellate the older adolescent. This practice has the avowed aim of charging him with semen. But here there are two purposes. One is to develop him into a warrior. The other is to enable him to carry out his duty as a sire when, on attaining adulthood, he is returned to the society of women (as well as men) and duly married. It may be added that despite his 'conditioning' by regular fellatio with older, then younger, men, he never returns to homosexuality.

The emphasis on semen might well lead one to suppose that the important goal was procreation. While the custom can be read that way and therefore be at odds with what I have said above, I doubt the correctness of the construction. For it would seem that the first objective of any (every) society must be defence. If the presumption sounds a bit a priori, the question might be raised: how would we set about structuring a society in which the first objective was to learn how to make a fire, or a dam, even though surrounded by hostile tribes — a very sophisticated social development would have to take place if the society were to create an army artificially, or hire mercenaries for protection while busy with other social developments.

But why is semen connected with soldiering at all? After all its structure does centre on fertilisation. Freud did not solve this problem; he simply placed an instinct of aggression beside that of sexuality. Why, then, have women not become warriors? There is a simple answer, to part of the question at least: women produce ova. Nurturing is incompatible with soldiering. So men have no choice; they must protect the nest and be the provider. Evolution would see to that. But we still lack an answer to what appears to result from anthropological researches, namely why semen seems to have as its first function, above that of insemination, that of providing men with a basis for soldiering.

The only guess I can make, and I make it without much confidence, is simplistic. Let us assume that geneticists can explain the basis of erectile tissue with the gonads playing a large part. Killing for many a long day depended on the knife. In the earliest days is must have depended on sheer physical strength. We can see both of these in terms of stiffness; and therefore see erection, having stemmed from the gonads, as the model underlying any form of stiffness needed for killing. Because of gonadal and penile involvement, it seems likely that men enjoyed killing. Stiffness, moreover, would also provide resistance to attack.

But even if this subsidiary answer to a subsidiary question is incorrect, it should not deflect our attention from the reasons why men fear being deprived by women of their manhood. To which there should be added the consequence that men look on women as trying to become men.

It is interesting to notice that it is impossible to discuss women at any length without also discussing something about men, and vice versa.

20

Review

Quibus dictis as Caesar would have said, I have to ask myself — or a percipient reader will — what they, these things, amount to.

Anyone going into some matter of psychodynamics has first to come to terms with whatever grains of gold are left from Freud after confusions, mistakes, adulations, and criticisms have been sorted out. This clearing of the ground has taken up most of part 1: the relation between the conscious and the unconscious was not new to Freud though the aspect discussed above may have been; and as for unconscious Phantasy, though the idea has been generally attributed to Melanie Klein, it was promulgated by Freud — in 1897 — when he gave up the theory of the reality of past traumata. The problems in Part 1 could have been dealt with at any time after Freud's death by any competent philosopher of science.

So we turned to bisexuality and homosexuality in part 2. When I first launched chapter 12, on male and female, as a paper, I thought that Freud's theory of bisexuality was false, which I have later had to retract in the light of anthropological and physiological evidence. As I now see the matter, bisexuality has to be included alongside my theory of androgyny; though I did think of it myself I came to realise I must have got it from Aristophanes and

Jung. Alas, when Fliess proposed it to Freud, Freud rejected it out of hand. I do not understand why he let a good idea slip through his fingers — perhaps it was too psychological at a time when Freud had great hopes of a neuro-physiological explanation of the neuroses, real science, hard science.

My view of androgyny was unlike Freud's theory in its further development. Freud's theory of male and of female sexuality led in a new direction, with no attempt to deal with the inscrutability of the nature of women which he openly admitted completely baffled him. I have provided some sort of answer, which necessitated a look at their counterpart, the nature of men, to which I also attempted to provide a new answer. There is not much in psycho-analytic literature about the discussions of the nature of women and men, but it is an analytic background that enabled me to put them in a new light; it is infused by Freudian thinking with a bow also towards the Jungians.

I have also made a fresh attempt to tackle the problem of homosexuality and the perversions; for I think it is time someone should tackle them head-on as a theoretical problem. Armed with a clinical observation of Freud's and one of Klein's theories, I have tried to do just this. It may be said — and it has been said — that my attempt is purely speculative.

Vale

It is around fifty years since I had my first contact with psychoanalysis in December 1933. My best discoveries came after I had retired when I was 71. One was the enormous value in almost any context of a background and training in philosophy: finding out where the problem lies, what is the centre of the problem, seeing what distinctions are relevant and need to be drawn, finding out what facts or factors or theories are relevant to the solution of the problem, elucidating these, and making a tentative assessment of what force there may be in them. Is it any wonder that I ended up realising I knew nothing?

Bion was at ease early at knowing nothing; I am not comfortable with it.

When philosophers become involved in a psychoanalytic discussion, they tend to dwell on matters of little importance to psychoanalysis; this may be due in part to their own nature. One could imagine a profitable meeting between Schopenhauer, Nietzsche, and Sartre. The International Psycho-Analytical Association missed a grand opportunity when its biennial meeting was held in Paris; instead of having an opening speech by the international president, the Association could have invited Jean-Paul Sartre to give an address. We know of course that he didn't believe in the unconscious — even Sir Karl believes in — and thought he could manage to do without it. I know a distinguished analyst who appears to think the same. I on the other hand continue to hold that Freud's two greatest discoveries were the dynamic Unconscious and Phantasy.

My concluding remark is to emphasize for the understanding of women, men, and society the importance of androgyny. Our great lost opportunity was that it was not developed by Plato, or Aristophanes himself, or by Freud. It was all implicit in my paper, 'Male and Female' (1983), but I did not realise it till long afterwards.

Having given papers to several component societies and published many papers on relatively minor matters, I realised that none of my few books was on psychoanalysis. So I thought I should write one; I feel I owe it to psychoanalysis to write one; also it is as good a way as any of passing the time between one's eightieth year and one's death. I made no plan for it but let it develop (I altered the initial position and made certain other decisive alterations of some chapters); and I shall not be offended if some readers say that that is how it reads. But my publisher has given some improved order to the chapters.

For most of my life I thought no one read me. Then a decade or so ago I discovered that three people made a point of reading me. A publisher's reader made a fourth. Another publisher's reader blacklisted me. I hope this book will be acceptable to my small public.

I want this book, since it is not scientific, to be evocative — or, to use a better term suggested by my friend Michael Gilbert, seminal.

Locutus sum.

References

Abraham, Karl (1922), 'A Short Study of the Development of the Libido', *Selected Papers on Psycho-Analysis*, Hogarth Press and Institute of Psycho-Analysis, London, 418–579.

Bail, Bernard, see Gorlick.

Bak, R. C. (1953), 'Fetishism', *J. Am. Psychonal. Assoc., 1*, 285–95.

Baker, I. (1977), 'Masculine and Feminine Psyches'. Lecture at the Analytical Psychology Society of Ontario, 25 March.

Balint, M. L. (1952), *Primary Love and Psycho-Analytic Technique*, Hogarth Press and Institute of Psycho-Analysis, London, esp. Ch. 8, esp. 152, also Balant's inspired phrase, 'dependent, idealised, identification' (155).

Bartley III, W. W. (1977), 'What Was Wrong with Darwin', *The New York Review of Books, 24*, 15 Sept. 34–36.

Bion, W. R. (1962), *'Experience in Groups'*, London: Tavistock.

Bion, W. R. (1967), *'Second Thoughts'*, Maresfield, London.

Blanchard & Freund, see Freund, Kurt (1982).

Bornstein, S. (1935), 'A Child Analysis', *Psychoanal. Q.* 4: 190–225.

Brenner, Charles (1955), "Validation of Psycho-analytic Technique", *J. Am. Psychoanal. Assoc.*, see Paul.

Bressler, B. (1961), A note on the bisexual significance of the testes. *Brit. J. Med. Psychol.*, 34: 277–280.

Deutsch, Helene (1925), Psychoanalyse der weiblicken Sexualfunktionen, *Wien*.

——— (1930), "The Significance of Masochism in the Mental Life of Women", *IPP-A, 11*, 48: originally in *Int. Z. Psychoanal., 16*, 172: "Masochismus und seine Beziehung zur Frigidistat".

——— (1933), "On Female Homosexuality", *Int. J. P-A, 14*, 34: originally (1932) in *Int. Z. Psychoanal., 18*, 219.

———— (1947), *"The Psychology of Women*, (1947), Research Books, 2 Vols., London.

Doi, L. Takeo (1962), "An Attempt at Reformulation of the Concept of Narcissism", unpublished — see other entry.

———— (1962), "Amae: a Key Concept for Understanding Japanese Cultural Structure, its Development and Characteristics", in Japanese Culture (1962), ed. by Smith & Beardsley.

———— (1962), "Attempt at Reformulation of the Concept of Narcissism", presented to the Annual Meeting of the American Psychoanalytical Assoc. cf. ("Some Thoughts on Helplessness and the Desire to be Loved", 1963), *Psychiatry, 26,* 266-272.

———— (1971), *Amae no Kozo Kobundo.* Tokyo. Translated as *The Anatomy of Dependence,* Harper & Row, New York, 1981; several editions & reprintings, most recent 1985.

———— (1989), "The Concept of Amae & its Psychoanalytic Implications", *Int. Rev. Psycho-Anal., 16,* 349-54.

———— (1990), "Introducing the Concept of Amae", *Papua New Guinea Med. J., 33,* 147-150.

Evans, W. H. (1951), Simulated Pregnancy in a Male, *Psychoanal. Q.,* 20: 165-178.

Ezriel, Henry (1956), "Experimentation within the Psychoanalytic Session", *B. J. Philos. Sc.* No. 25, 29-48.

Fairbairn, W. R. D. (1952), *Psychoanalytic Studies of the Personality,* Tavistock, London.

Feinbloom, D. (1976), "Transvestites and Trans-sexuals". New York: Delta.

Fenichel, Otto (1945), 'The Psychoanalytic Theory of Neurosis', New York.

Fordham, M. (1984), Personal Communication.

Freeman, T. (1951), 'Pregnancy as a Precipitant of Mental Illness in Men', *Brit. J. Med. Psychol.,* 24: 49-54.

Freud, S. (1895), *'Studies on Hysteria', Stand. Ed., 2.*

———— (1905), *'Three Essays on the Theory of Sexuality', Stand. Ed., 7,* 123-43.

———— (1908), *'On the Sexual Theories of Children', Stand. Ed., 9.*

———— (1922), *'Beyond the Pleasure — Principle, Stand. Ed., 18.*

———— (1923), *'The Ego [The Id.,* Hogarth Press & Inst. of Psycho-Analysis, London, *Stand. Ed., 19,* (1961).

———— (1925), *'An Autobiographical Study', Stand. Ed., 20,* 42-3.

———— (1936), *'An Outline of Psycho-Analysis', Stand. Ed., 23,* pp. 202-3.

———— (1937), *'Constructions in Analysis', Stand. Ed., 23.*

Freund, Kurt (1982a), 'Experimental Analysis of Pedophilia', *Behav. Res. Theory, 20,* 105-12, esp. 112.

———— (1982b), 'Two Types of Cross-Gender Identity', *Arch. Sex. Behaviour, 11,* pp. 49-63, 60.

———— (1983), 'The Courtship Disorders', *Arch. Sex. Behav., 12,* 369, 79.

————, Blanshard, R. (1983), 'Measuring Masculine Gender Identity in Females', *J. Consulting & Clinical Psychology, 51,* pp. 205-14.

———— (1985), 'Cross-Gender Identity in a Broder Context', *Gender Pysphora,* (ed. Steiner), New York. Plenum, pp. 259-324.

Friedman, J. & Gasser, S. (1951), "Orestes", *Psychoanal. Q.,* 20: 423-433.

Frisch, O. R. (1963), 'The Magnetic Proton', *Listener*, 459–60.

Galenson, E. (1976), 'Some Suggested Revisions Concerning Early Female Development', *J. Am. Psychoanalytic Assoc., 24*, 20–57.

Gillespie, W. H. (1952), 'Notes on the Analysis of Sexual Perversion', *Int. J. Psycho-Analysis, 33*, pp. 297–402.

_____ (1956), 'The General Theory of the Sexual Perversion', *Int. J. Psycho-Analysis, 37*.

_____ (1964), 'Symposium on Homosexuality', *Int. J. Psycho-Analysis, 45*, pp. 203–9.

Gorlick, Loraine A. & Bail Bernard (1989), Personal Communication.

Greenson, R. R. (1964), 'On Homosexuality and Gender Identity', *Int. J. Psychoanal, 45*: 217–219.

Grosskurth, Phyllis (1986), *'Melanie Klein, Her World and Her Work'*, McClelland & Stewart.

_____ (1980), *Havelock Ellis: A Biography,* Allen & Lane, London.

_____ (1964), *John Addington Symonds: The Woeful Victorian, A Biography*, Longman, London.

Guntrip, Harry (1961), *Personality Structure and Human Interaction: The Developing Synthesis of Psychodynamic Theory*, London: The Hogarth Press and the Institute of Psycho-Analysis.

Hardin, H. (1984), Personal Communication.

_____ (1987), 'On The Vicissitudes of Freud's Early Mothering: (1) Early Environment & Loss', *Psychoanalytic Quarterly, 56*, 628–44; (1988) Part 2: Alienation from his Biological Mother, *Same, 57*, 72–86.

Hattiangadi, J. N. (1987), *'How Is Language Possible?'*, LaSalle, Illinois.

Hayman, Anne (1987), 'What do We Mean by Phantasy?', *Bull. of Brit. Psycho-Analytical Soc.,* London.

Heimann, Paula, see Isaacs.

_____ (1952), 'Certain Functions of Introjection & Projection on Early Infancy', Chap. 4; see also Chapters 5 & 10 in Isaacs (1952).

Hendrick, I. (1933), 'Pregenital Anxiety in a Passive Feminine Character', *Psychoanal, Q.*, 2: 68–93.

Homburger, E. (1935), 'Psychoanalysis and The Future of Education', *Psychoanal, Q.*, 4: 50–68.

Horney, Karen (1924), 'On the Genesis of the Castration-Complex in Women', *Int. J. Psycho-Anal., 5*, 50; German Edition (*Zeitscrift*) a year earlier.

_____ (1926), 'Flight from Womanhood', *Int. J. Psycho-Anal., 7*: Same in *Zeitscrift, 12*.

Isaacs, Susan (1939), 'Criteria for Interpretation', *Int. J. Psycho-Anal., 20*, 148.

_____ (1952), 'The Nature and Function of Phantasy', in Klein, Melanie, Heimann, Paula, Isaacs, Susan, and Riviere, Joan, Hogarth Press & Institute of Psycho-Analysis, London, 67–121. Isaacs' paper appeared originally, same title, *Int. J. Psycho-Anal., 29*, 73–97.

Jarvie, I. C. (1964), 'The Revolution in Anthropology', New York The Humanities Press, New York

_____ (1973), 'Functionalism, Burgess, Minneapolis.

_____ (1984), 'Rationalism & Relativism' in search of a Philosophy & History of Anthropology, Routledge & Kegan Paul, London.

Jones, Earnest (1927), 'The Early Development of Female Sexuality', *Int. J. Psycho-Anal., 8,* 489: also in Jones (1951).

Jones, Ernest (1948), "Anal-Erotic Character Traits", *Papers on Psycho-Analysis,* 5th ed. 413-37, Baillièr, Tindal, & Cox, London.

Kapp, R. O. (1962), Personal Communication.

Kempf, E. J. (1945, 1946), 'Ontogany of Bisexual Differentiation in Man', in selected papers, ed. by Kempf, Dorothy & Burnham, J. C. Indiana University Press, Bloomington & London, 110-302.

Klein, M. (1921), 'The Development of a Child' in *Contributions to Psycho-Analysis,* 1921-45. London. Hogarth, pp. 56-7.

———— (1923), 'Infant Analysis', in *Contribution to Psycho-Analysis,* 1921-45. London. Hogarth, p. 97.

———— (1932), 'The Psycho-Analysis of Children'. London. Hogarth, p. 190.

———— (1945), 'The Oedipus Complex in the Light of Early Anxieties' in Contributions to Psycho-Analysis, 1921-45. London. Hogarth, p. 360.

———— (1946), 'Notes on Some Schiznid Mechanisms', in Isaacs, (1948).

———— (1957), 'Envy and Gratitude', London Tavistock.

Körner, S. (1964), 'Deductive Unification and Idealisation', *British Journal of Phil. Sci. 14.*

Kubie, L. S. (1952), 'Problems and Techniques of Psycho-Analytic Validation and Progress', *Psychoanalysis as Science,* ed. Pumpian-Mindlin, Stanford U. Press.

Kuperman, Maurice (1979), 'A Critique of Freud's Theory Of Malaise of Civilization', Ph. D. Dissertation, Library of York University, Toronto.

Lakatos, Imre (1963-4), 'Proofs and Refutations', *Brits. J. Philos. Sc., 14.*

Lampl De Groot, J. (1933), 'Problems of Femininity', *Psychoanal, Q.,* 2: 489-518.

Lewin, B. D. (1933), 'The Body as Phallus', *Psychoanal, Q.,* 2: 24-47.

Lewinsky, H. (1952), 'Features from a case of Homosexuality', *Psychoanal, Q.,* 21: 344-354.

Limentani, A. (1979), 'The Significance of Trans-sexualism in Relation to Some Basic Psychoanalytic Concepts. *Int. Rev. Psychoanal., 6:* 139-153.

Lorenz, Konrad (1967), 'On Aggression', London: Methuen & Co. Ltd.

McDougall, Joyce (1989), 'The Dead Father', *Int. J. Psycho-Anal., 70,* 205-20.

Mahler, M. S., Pine, F., & Bergmann, A. (1975), 'The Psychoanalytic Birth of the Human Infant', New York, Basic Books.

Masson, Jeffrey, (1984), *The Assault on Truth,* Farrar, Strauss and Giroux, New York.

Matte-Blanko, Ignatio (1981), 'Reflecting with Bion', in Grotstein, James S. (ed.), *Do I Dare Disturb the Universe? A Memorial to Wilfred R. Bion,* Beverly Hills: Caesura Press.

May, W. F. (1974), 'Terrorism as Strategy and Ecstasy', *Soc. Res.* Summer, 277-98.

Medawar, Sir P. (1963), 'Is the Scientific Paper a Fraud?', *Listener, 12,* 377-8.

———— (1967), 'Darwin's Illness', in *The Art of The Soluble,* London, pp. 61-70.

Meltzer, D. (1968), 'Parapersecution Dread', *Int. J. Psycho-Analysis, 49,* 396-400.

Money, John (1970-71), 'Sex Reassignment', *J. Psychiat, 9:* 249-269.

Murdock, Iris (1986), 'The Good Apprentice', Chatto & Wandus, London, 339-341, (the passages in Bion that resemble Murdock's are in F. Bion (ed.) (1980)

Bion in New York and San Paulo, Roland Harris Trust, Clung; F. Bion (ed.) (1987), Clinic Seminars Brasilia & San Paulo & Four Papers, Fleetwood Press, Abingdon.

O'Gorman, F. P. (1977), 'Poincaré's Conventionalism of Applied Geometry', *Stud. Hist. Philos. of Science, 8*, 303–40.

O'Shaughnessy, E. (1955), 'Can a Liar be Psycho-Analysed?', *Brit. Psycho-Analytical Soc. Bull.*, No. 4, April 1–14.

Paul, Louis (1963), 'Psychoanalytic Clinical Interpretation', New York.

Phillips, Adam (1988), *Winnicott*. Cambridge (Mass.): Harvard University Press.

Plaut, A. (1953), 'On the Clinical Importance of the Hermaphrodite', *Brit. J. Med. Psychol., 26*: 133–139.

Popper, K. R. (1959), *The Logic of Scientific Discovery*, Hutchinson, London.

_____ (1983), *Postscript to The Logic of Scientific Discovery*, Hutchinson, London, in section "A Case of Verificationism", Vol. 1, 163–74.

_____ (1983), 'Realism and the Aims of Science' in Vol. 1 of the *Postscript to the Logic of Scientific Discovery*', ed. W. W. Bartley III, London: Hutchinson.

Rado, S. (1933), 'Fear of Castration in Women', *Psychoanal. Q.*, 2: 425–488.

Roazen, Paul (1985), *Helene Deutsch, a Psycho-Analyst's Life*, Garden City, New York: Anchor Press/Doubleday.

Roazen, P. (1983), 'As If & Politics', *Political Psycho., 4*, pp. 685, 92.

_____ (1990), 'Review of Krell', *J. Hist. Behav. Sciences, 26*, 197.

Rosenfelt, Herbert (1965), *Psychotic States*, New York: Inter-Universities Press.

Rycroft, C. (1955), Personal Communication.

Rycroft, C. (1984), 'A Case of Hysteria', *New York Review of Books, 31*, No. 6, 3–6.

Scott, W. C. M. (1946), 'On the Intense Affects Encountered in Treating a Severe Manic-Depressive Disorder', *Int. J. Psycho-Analysis, 28*.

_____ (1980), 'Narcissism, The Body, Phantasy, Fantasy, Internal & External Objects and the Body Scheme'. Meeting of Advanced Inst. Analytic Psycho-therapy. New York. May 16.

_____ (1981), 'The Development of the Analysands' Enthusiasm for the Process of Analysis', see Grotstein (1981).

_____ (1985), Personal Communication.

Seaborn Jones, G. (1961), 'Some Philosophical Implications of Psycho-Analysis', *Int. J. Psycho-Analysis*, Ph.D. Thesis, Univ. of London.

Segal, Hanna (1986), 'A Note on Symbol-Formation', *Delusion & Creativity & other Essays*, Free Associations, London, 49.

Strachey, James (1934), 'The Nature of the Therapeutic Action in Psycho-Analysis', *Int. J. Psycho-Anal.*, see Paul (1963).

Stroller, R. J. (1964), 'A Contribution to the Study of Gender Identity', *Int. J. Psychoanal., 45*: 220–226.

_____ (1965), 'The Sense of Maleness'.

_____ (1968), *Sex and Gender*, London: Hogarth.

_____ (1974), 'Hostility and Mystery in Perversion', *Int. J. Psycho-Analysis, 45*, 425–34.

_____ (1974), 'Symbiosis Anxiety and the Development of Masculinity', *Archives of Gen. Psychiatry, 30*, 164–72.

_____ (1975), *The Trans-sexual Experiment*, Hogarth, London.

_____ (1976), *Perversion: The Erotic Form of Hatred*, London. Harvester.

———— (1984), 'La Perversion et le Désir de Faire Mal'. La Chose Sexuelle, Nouvelle revue de psychanalyse. Paris, *Gallimard, 29*, 147–71.

———— (1985), *Observing the Erotic Imagination*, New York and London: Yale University Press, esp. 108–17.

———— (1985), *Presentations of Gender*, New York and London: Yale University Press, esp. 108–17.

Sulloway, Frank J. (1979), *Freud, Biologist of The Mind, Beyond the Psychoanalytic Level*, New York: Basic Books, 1979.

Warnes, Hector (1945), 'A Particular Type of Perverse Marital Relationship', *Psychiatric J. of the Univ. of Ottawa, 11*, 32–4.

Watkins, J. W. N. (1957), 'Between Analytic & Empirical', *Philo., 32*, 130.

Watkins, J. W. N. (1958), 'Confirmable & Influential Metaphysics', *Mind, 67*.

Wilson, G. W. (1948), 'A Further Contribution to the Study of Olfactory Repression with Particular Reference to Transvestitism', *Psychoanal. Q.*, 17: 322–339.

Winslow, J. H. (1971), 'Darwin's Victorian Malady: Evidence for Its Medically Induced Origin', *Amer. Philos. Soc.*, Philadelphia.

Wisdom, J. O. (1946),

———— (1954), 'Is Epiphenomenism Refutable?', *Proc. 2nd Inter. Congr. Philos. Sc.*, Neuchatel, Zürich.

———— (1956), 'Psycho-Analytical Technology', *B. J. Philos. Sc., 7*.

———— (1960), 'Some Main Mind-Body Problems', *Proc. Arist. Soc., 60*, 201–7.

———— (1961), 'Respect for Persons, the Pleasure Principle & Obligation', *Proc. XII Inter. Congr. Philos., Firenzi, 7*.

———— (1961), 'A Methodological Approach to the Problem of Hysteria', *Int. J. Psycho-Analysis, 42*, 231–2.

———— (1962), 'Criteria for a Psycho-Analytic Interpretation', *Proc. Arist. Soc., Sup. Vol. 36*, 101–3.

———— (1962), 'Comparison & Development of the Psycho-Analytic Theories of Melancholic', *Int. J. Psycho-Analysis, 43*, 113–32.

———— (1964), 'A Methodological Approach to the Problem of Obsessional Neurosis', *Brit. J. Med. Psychol.*, 37: 111–131.

———— (1965), 'Anti-Dualist Outlook and Social Enquiry', in Colloquium for Philosophy of Science, 1965, North Holland Publishing Co., Amsterdam, 1968, Vol. 3. Edited by Lakatos and Musgrave, London.

———— (1966), 'What is the explanatory Theory of Obsessional Neurosis?', *Brit. J. Med. Psychol.*, 39: 335–48.

———— (1966), 'Testing a Psycho-Analytic Interpretation', *Ratio, 8*, 55–76.

———— (1967), 'Testing an Interpretation within a Session', shortened version of 1966 paper in *Ratio, Int. J. Psycho-Analysis*.

———— (1968), 'Anti-Dualist Outlook & Social Enquiry Problems in the Philosophy of Science', *Proc. Intern. Colloquium* (1965) Vol. 3, Ed. Musgrave & Lakatos.

Wisdom, J. O. (1983), 'Male and Female', *Int. J. Psycho-Analysis, 64*, 159–68.

———— (1983), 'Darwin's Chronic Illness', *Philos. Social Sc., 14*, 169–71.

———— (1984), 'What is Left of Psycho-Analytic Theory?', *Int. Rev. Psycho-Analysis, 11*, 303–26.

———— (1985), 'The Psychic Structure of Havelock Ellis'. *Int. Rev. Psycho-Analysis, 65*, 413–5.

_____ (1986), 'Trauma or Intrapsychic Conflict?', *Phil. Soc. Sci., 16*, 135–40.
_____ (1987), *Challengeability in Modern Science*, Avebury, Aldershot.
_____ (1988), 'The Perversions: A Philosopher Reflects', *J. of Analytical Psychology, 33*, 229–248.
Zweig, Steven (1989), 'The Burning Secret and Other Stories', Cape, London.

Index

Plato, 74, 86
Plaut, A., 85
Popper, K., 4, 5
Power, 15, 120
Pragmatism, 117
Preconscious, 5
Preconscious fantasy, 46
Preconscious trauma, 45
Predictable defence, 42
Presence of listener, 4, 78
Pressure method, 4
Primary Narcissism, 30
Projective identification, 6, 7, 92, 98
Pseudocyesis, 99
Psychoanalysis as psychology of the
    unconscious, 45, 46
Psychoanalysis as science, vii
Psychology of the Japanese, 24
Psychoses, 18, 30
Punishment, 54, 55
Punishment-need fulfilment, 55
Punishment needs, 52, 60, 61, 62, 63,
    64, 65, 66n

Q year for reproduction, 171

Rape, 129
Reaction-formation, 56
Repression, 6
Research case, 5
Resistance, 4
Rickman, 55
Roazen, P., vii, viii
Rosenfelt, Huhut, 18
Rycroft, C., 5

Sadism, 27, 56, 67, 81, 82
Sartre, J-P., 36, 66, 135
Satan, 6
Schizophrenic, 30, 79, 135
Schreiner, Olive, 89
Scott, W. C. M., 18, 46, 106n, 128,
    135
Secondary elaboration, 62, 64, 65,
    77
Segal, H., 14, 18, 46
Semen and soldiering, 130
Semen for warrior, 229
Sense of guilt, 47

Sewerage system, 15
Sex instinct, 17
Sexual drive, 17, 18
Sexual libido, 17, 19, 21
Sexual lust, 17
Shame, 24
Shaw, B., 76, 127
Silberer, 63
Siva, 10
Social relations as anatomical, 75
Socrates, 6
Speculation, viii
Stengel, 15
Stevin of Bruges, vii
Stoller, R., viii, 85, 103, 115, 125, 127
Strachey, James, 3
Sublimation, 14, 36, 45
Sulloway, Frank J., 17
Superego, 19, 20, 35, 40
Superego, as terrorist, 19, 20
Symbolization, 55, 60, 65, 77
Symbols, 13, 14
Symptoms, 5

Thorner, H., v, 11, 22, 25
Threshold dreams, 6
Toilet training, 28
Transference, 48, 77
Transference, negative, 4, 5
Transference, positive, 4
Transformation to anal phase, 19
Trauma, 5, 40
Trauma-re-enactment dreams, 51f
Two-body psychology, 22, 30
Two-body theories, 116

Unconscious, 38, 41, 42, 48, 135
Unconscious, as 'pushed back', 39,
    45, 46
Unconscious Phantasy, 46, 132
Unconscious Punishment-need, 51
University of Toronto, 112
Unpleasure, 52

Victorianism, 11, 17, 97

Warnes, H., 95
Weltanschauungen, 116
Whole object, 37